Restless Mind, Quiet Thoughts

Restless Mind, Quiet Thoughts

A Personal Journal

by PAUL EPPINGER

With Charles Eppinger, His Father

WHITE CLOUD PRESS
ASHLAND, OREGON

99 98 97 96 95 94   5 4 3 2 1

Cover design by Daniel Cook
Cover photography © Mark Woodhead
Printed in the United States of America

Photography credits:
Frontispiece and page 91 © by Christopher Nisperos
All other photographs from the collection of Charles Eppinger

LIBRARY OF CONGRESS CATALOGING IN PUBLICATION DATA

Eppinger, Paul
    Restless mind, quiet thoughts: a personal journal / by Paul Eppinger with Charles Eppinger
        p.   cm.
    ISBN 1-883991-07-2 : $12.95
    1. Eppinger, Paul   . 2. Suicide victims--United States-
Biography. 3. Eppinger, Paul   -- Correspondence.
4. Eppinger, Charles, --   Correspondence.   5. Fathers and sons--United States. I. Eppinger, Charles, .II. Title.
HV6548.U5E67   1994
362.2'8'092--dc20
[B]   94-26201
                                         CIP

For Leslie

TABLE OF CONTENTS

I wanted only to try to live in accord with the promptings which came from my true self. Why was that so very difficult?

Hermann Hesse, *Demian*

PREFACE

My son doesn't live anymore, not in the usual sense—but he does indeed live for me, and vividly, through his words and thoughts, through the unusual insights that he often possessed. So I've decided to preserve them, and to share them. From his journals, his letters to me, his other occasional writings: these all coalesce into the account of a thoughtful journey by a thoughtful young man, through the years of his third decade.

It was a time of serious, diligent searching: for an understanding of this complex life—of what our culture has shaped it into—of how an individual with integrity and sensitivity can discover, or create, a way of fitting into it, and perhaps of making a contribution. Paul loved this earth; he loved life. But he was often baffled by the ways of our species: by the many futile, sometimes tragic, directions taken in our attempts to live effectively with the earth, with its creatures, with each other.

He sensed, deep inside himself, that there must be a natural, a right way to exist on this planet. In art, in music, in nature he constantly saw beauty, and worth, and truth. He hoped somehow to translate these promptings into the skills of successful living. But noting the expectations of society, watching the lives of others around him, he could find little to guide him toward this rightness. We all feel this tug toward such fulfillment, but Paul seemed to sense it more intensely than most. He once said, "Man has other basic needs than food, warmth, and shelter; we need love, expression, and truth. We must not allow ourselves to believe that we can fill the round hole of our spirit with the square peg of objective rationale."

He responded to these yearnings with his considerable powers of intellect and intuition; he didn't presume to provide answers to the great unanswerable questions—those seemingly remote cosmic issues that some-

how turn out to powerfully affect our daily lives; nor did he try to define the meaning of life in the abstract. His sights were set at a more modest distance. His ponderings were honest reflections on his life and how he felt about his world and relationships. If they can cause us to think more deeply about our own lives, to wonder more often what it's all about, then he will have made at least a portion of that longed-for contribution.

He never set out to teach me anything, but I gained a multitude of precious understandings from my exchanges with him—both the audible and the silent kinds. He was a person of superb sensory appreciation: when he listened to music, ate a good meal, felt the sun on his back, or watched the clouds move across the sky, Paul savored the experience of that moment like no one else I've ever known. He also had a playful, sometimes mischievous, side—showing itself in his sense of humor and the ability to not always take himself too seriously. I was exceedingly fortunate to know him closely, and to share, with him, an exquisite love—a love which eventually became more like that of dear friends, than of father and son.

Many times during this project, as I labored with his words, I found myself typing through tear-blurred vision as I saw Paul's deepest self, poured out onto those pages. My perception is that his observations and opinions were often profound; my hope is that you will be moved to reread, slowly and patiently, portions of his writings which sometimes reveal new and deeper meanings and nuances as the words are mulled over.

I have not attempted to homogenize Paul's various writings, by modifying tense, person, and the other mechanical components of proper syntax. These words were mostly set down for his private use—without thinking another person would ever see them; some were scribbled in real time (ofttimes in the darkness of the wee-hours), some in retrospect. But they all deserve to be seen in the original, so as to preserve their true flavor.

In order to make it clear that the words presented are mine, they will be italicized like those in this paragraph. When the words and thoughts are Paul's, they will be set forth like those in the next paragraph, taken from one of his journals.

Preface

In a dream, I noticed on the table a manuscript written by Dad. Its title implied that he had written down all of his thoughts and impressions of me. I was very excited to read it.

As with each of us, Paul did not experience the cavalcade of his days with smoothness and consistency: some days were good, some definitely weren't. Some days he felt like writing; some days he didn't. These apparent contradictions don't betray a weakness in his character, as I perceive the human experience. On the contrary, they signal an openness, a willingness to be seen as one really is, to admit the reality of an emotion, to act as one feels. Without this sort of "contradiction" in a journal, we should not trust the honesty of the words—however fine.

Here, then, is the story of my son's special journey, and of my connection with it.

Charles Eppinger

Beginnings

The First Nineteen Years

Shortly after my birth we moved to Denver, into a stark and unimaginative neighborhood of middle-class cracker-box tract houses. There was little life there: few trees or lawns, little variation between houses. Everything was new, and cheap. The neighborhood was constantly changing, and very unsettling as people came and went quickly. I remember very little from this time, and none of it is good.

We lived in this bleakness for five years, at which point we moved into an older and much more established neighborhood in northeast Denver. Here the houses were large, with lots of character and history. Tall trees, lots of parks and lawns, birds and squirrels and butterflies. It was much more conducive to the temperament of a little boy (or anyone else, for that matter), and I'll always remember *it* as the place that I grew up in. The house itself was large and friendly, and I gave my imagination full rein, exploring and playing and fantasizing.

My family did almost everything together: cooking and eating meals, weekends working around the house and yard, or driving through the mountains. Usually, wherever my parents went, my sister Leslie and I were expected to go. I was also required to participate in certain events. Church, of course, and many times a week. I was given piano lessons by my father, and was made to participate in public recitals. Also, for many years, I played little league football and base-ball, constantly being exposed to the brutal anger of a terrifying and tyrannical coach.

I learned how to read and write early, and spent most of my alone time submerged in books, or writing little stories. But some of my solitary time was spent endlessly exploring outside. I was fasci-nated by animals, and spent long hours chasing birds, butterflies, bees, squirrels—and cutting pictures of animals out of books and magazines. I always had a small menagerie of turtles, hamsters, and other interesting creatures.

Grade school was traumatic for me. I was shy and submissive, and had to make a great effort to speak out in class, or to other students. I was usually in the advanced classes, a role which made me somewhat uncomfortable. Until the age of ten or so, I had problems speaking; I tended to mumble and run my words together, so I had weekly lessons at home with a speech therapist.

Being left handed, I also had trouble writing correctly. My brain wanted to write one way; my teachers wanted me to write another. I had to spend extra time at home, practicing penmanship, and this caused a lot of frustration.

At age eleven we moved again, to a large, very modern house in the suburbs at the southeast edge of town. It was gut-wrenching to leave the old friendly house and neighborhood, but I soon adapted once again to the sterile existence of suburban life.

By the beginning of his teens, Paul had survived the breakup of my marriage with his mother, what he perceived as my abandonment of him and his sister, and the presence of new mates for both parents—all in addition to the usual pressures of advancing adolescence. He lived with his sister, his mother, and her new husband. His life, already, had in-cluded having his home dislocated five times, by the age of fourteen.

Things between me and each of my parents degenerated badly from this time. My mother seemed totally beyond coping with the demands of her new situation and I hated her new husband. My father had a fresh set of distractions (including a new wife—whom I also hated) to keep him from bothering with me. I felt like I was on my own from about age twelve.

I began junior high, and for the first time, was able to surround myself with a large and closely knit circle of friends. We were a somewhat radical group, and involved ourselves in anything we thought implied rebellion: philosophies, politics, fashion, crime, and involvement with drugs. This drug use continued for more than six years, and probably made a significant contribution to my perception of the world.

About the same time, I began spending my summers in the wilds of northwest Colorado. There was a man who ran a wilderness training program there, and I began as a participant for several weeks each summer, eventually being hired on and spending my entire summer months, and part of the fall, guiding backpacking and hunting trips. I sometimes look at this as my saving grace: time spent in the forest, away from family and the city, with a very healthy atmosphere of work and intimate social involvement. It was through these experiences that I began to develop a self-image—my *own*.

As he began to discover more and more pieces of a self, largely obscured in early life by the pressures of parents, school, church, and many other symbols of authority—of repression, Paul also found that this inner self contained the seeds of anxiety, of uncertainty. As with many sixteen-year-olds, it became a time of alienation, of experimentation—of groping and stumbling. And then. . .

It was Sunday the end of afternoon, and after having been kicked out of the house three weeks or so before, and living with friends, in my car, or with Leslie at college, I came home. I got in a terrible fight with my mother—the worst, most obscene and physical I'd ever had. I got extremely upset, and packed all my valuable possessions and clothes, with her standing, watching. I stormed out of the house and got on the highway intending to see my sister in Fort Collins. I was in a frightful rage.

Then the idea of suicide occurred. I calmed down immediately. I had been thinking seriously of doing myself in for many months, and had bought a hundred reds (Seconal) with the thought coming to mind often.

I drove to Cherry Creek Reservoir and stopped in a secluded area for campers. There were four or five close by, but I thought little of them. I did the reds two at a time, at intervals gauged to about fifteen minutes. I did this because I was afraid if I did them all at once, I would either throw them up, or suffocate. The whole time I was doing this, it all seemed very unreal. But I was ecstatic that I was finally doing it.

I was getting very high, having a hard time breathing, seeing, or hearing. I urinated extensively several times. I sat in my car, leaving only to piss. I wrapped a blanket around me, and sat stretched out, giggling, and talked loudly to myself. I also smoked a great deal of Columbo pot. At this time, becoming drowsy, I took what drugs I had and stashed them in the paneling of my car door. My reasoning behind this action was vague, but I thought that my friends knew I kept dope there, so if they ever got into my car, they might check. A nice present.

I tried to think how many I took. The number 9 stuck in my mind, so I wrote on the dash "9, not many". I also wrote on a check in the glove box, "Les, I'm thinking of you." My last remembrance was of looking at my watch: 7:00. It would be safe to assume I lost consciousness before 8:00. One final remembrance, which came to me days later: I remember getting out of my car, probably to piss, and having no sense of balance. I staggered about twenty yards, walking into the ground five or ten times and cutting my face and hands badly. I crawled back to the car. I don't know if this happened before I passed out, while I was unconscious, or soon after I awoke, being in a tremendous stupor.

I awoke Monday afternoon about 2:00 or 3:00.

What trauma, for a parent, can compare with the impact of a teenage suicide attempt? I was shocked, saddened, terrified, supremely confused—all but immobilized. Looking back, I think I did not handle my responsibilities as a father with any real understanding or wisdom. Although I had grave reservations about the profession of psychiatry as a

whole, I couldn't find any sensible sounding alternative to the recom-
mendation of the psychiatrist—the "expert."

Confused and frightened by my act, my father committed me to
Mount Airy Psychiatric Hospital. I spent my first night there strapped
to a bed in a padded room with iron bars over the windows and light
bulbs.

It was while in Mount Airy that I began to exhibit anorexic behavior, allowing myself very little food, vomiting when I felt I'd
overeaten, and putting myself through a rigid regimen of exercise. My
body image became very distorted, and I just wanted to get skinnier
and skinnier. Though I was released after only six weeks, this episode
proved to be somewhat of a turning point in my view of my life, and
of myself. I could no longer ignore the possibility that there was something very wrong inside of me. The world, and especially my own
father, had apparently branded me insane. It didn't seem right.

After leaving Mount Airy, I moved to Fort Collins to finish high
school, and to live with my sister, who was attending college there.
There was no way in the world I could have returned to my mother's
house.

As Paul struggled to get himself together after a series of such ex-
treme traumas in his teen-age life, I began to reach for something more
in my own life. With only vague feelings that things were not right inside
me—that my health, my well-being, my behavior, my relationships were
not what they should or could be, I sought, in several directions, for a
path to take—with insignificant success. Finally, about the time Paul
moved to Fort Collins, I decided to undertake Primal Therapy.

I was into my final year of high school in Fort Collins, again
involving myself with a close group of friends. For the first time I was
able to assert leadership in a group of people; I was a boy from the
city, with his own house, and I was highly looked up to. Again, this
was a time of heavy drug use. Also during this time, I began stealing
occasionally, mostly burglarizing houses. And I served a short, token
jail sentence for this.

One day my father told me about Primal Therapy. It interested me extremely, even excited me. My father's change surprised me and made me very happy—hopeful for myself. Earlier that day I had been getting down, so I blocked it by becoming numb, irritated easily. But after my father's visit I was very happy. Then I saw some of the wrong people, smoked too much pot, worried over classes, and got very black. I tried my father's partial explanation of Primal, but all I could get was, when I closed my eyes, an image of a large round object, snowball maybe, being hurled directly at my face. This caused great anxiety and agitation, so I quit.

But then I started thinking of friends, and memories, of beautiful places and experiences. It made me very sad, lonely—partly because I'm terribly afraid I'll forget all these people and places and times, (or they'll forget me) and partly because I shouldn't be down about such things. I should have joy that I've lived such full glorious experiences. And I don't want to lose the feel for them.

Paul made a second attempt to end his life with another overdose of Seconal. This time he was more knowledgeable about what constituted a lethal dosage; he was comatose for five days, and hospitalized for more than a week with acute barbiturate poisoning. The skin on each of his extremities erupted from the severe reaction. But, amazingly, his overall health and stamina pulled him through an ordeal which had almost always proved fatal, in other cases.

At this point, my father, who was several months into Primal Therapy, and temporarily separated from his second wife, rented a small house in Denver and asked me to live with him. It was at this time that we began to renew our relationship. Because of the rawness of both our lives, we were able to begin to develop and share a deep understanding of each other.

It was a tentative, gradual healing of our connection, and filled with uncertainty. At one point, I recorded in my own journal: "Paul seems often like the walking dead—and he just wants to get honest about it, to complete it." Looking over old photos of him taken during this period, is very painful to me. I had no clear idea, at all, of where he was, of where we were, headed. All I could hold onto was a weak, vague sense of hope. But we kept at it, often clumsily. Neither of us had any other choices. I felt that Paul simply had to live with me—for a while—if he was to survive. Thankfully, we did make gradual progress in our relationship.

Then, after about six months of living with Paul, I was reunited with my wife, and Paul decided to move on—out on his own again. It was time.

I've been feeling OK. I've found a center which is neither good or bad or satisfying, but it keeps me from being distracted in my attempts to figure out my way. Though sometimes it almost feels like things are coming too easily; I'm always afraid of deceiving myself, as so many people do, into believing I'm headed towards the right path. The world is a very confusing thing, and my comprehension of it has barely scratched the surface. There is so much to say, and to ask.

Take to the Highway
The Twentieth & Twenty-first Years

The following fall I started college in southwest Colorado. It was a frightening move for me, but the newness, and the distance from my past helped me to repress my previous pain to some degree, and I was able to start a new life, and begin developing on my own. It was here that I was finally able to begin to experience myself. For a while, my drug use, anorexia and suicidal wishes disappeared, as I explored new and exciting ways of expressing myself, including beginning to keep a personal journal.

· · · · · · ·

I feel like I'm hiding out down in Durango now—attending Fort Lewis College. I guess I enjoy it. It's hard though after a summer of travel and hoboing and hopping freight trains and seeing many new and beautiful sights and people, and having outrageous adventures, to settle down once again; to have to look at clocks, have people tell you what to do and when; to wait till you have free time to do the things you want, and then no longer feel like doing them.

But I'm taking good advantage of it. I have a nice little home, off-campus, with Ned, a Ute Indian. We have plum and pear and apple trees and a small garden, so I've been baking pies a lot. I find Durango a beautiful town. Most students live up at the college, thank God, so I don't have to be involved in that kind of unwelcome environment.

The San Juan Mountains surround me here, plenty of beautiful places to hike or fish or bicycle.

The school is only about three thousand students, so classes and just the general feeling is very friendly. I love the drawing class I'm taking from a very warm and sensitive man, much like my father, and I'm happy with my work so far. And I'm taking Indian Arts from a Navajo woman born sometime before 1900— she doesn't know exactly when. I've been making baskets from corn husks. Geology is my only hard class, but it should prove to be interesting. Super-naturalism, required for freshman English, but a very open type class. Coed volleyball, just a chance to watch the pretty girls in their gym shorts.

All in all, a very good schedule for me. A fair amount of free time, personal classes and subjects, and a very fine atmosphere to hibernate the winter through.

· · · · · · ·

It's becoming an obsession now—jumping in the river every day— the best cure I know of for the blahs, or a hangover, or a foggy brain. I like doing it before a test, or some type of uncomfortable confrontation, or especially before making love. It is a perfect centering device, for clarity of mind and composure—to say nothing of the physical sense of awareness. It brings balance—better than eight hours of sleep or an hour of intense meditation.

Yet I wonder where it's leading me. Once the idea occurs to me I can't turn it down. You have to be a little loony to wake up at three in the morning, when it's ten degrees out, and just jump into the Animas River, with ice all around, on a cloudy day.

It has given me immense confidence in my self control, though, and I'll do it every day for as long as I'm near water and have the strength to fall in. Lo the day they find a blue body floating down the Animas with a big smile and three Adam's apples!

. . . .

Doubt and indecision will weaken any effort. It is best to work from one's first impulses—thus developing faith in one's innermost feelings and judgment. Thought and creativity can then happen as a flow. For when one flows, less energy is used up doing things, and progress is quickened—smoothed out. Then more energy can be used in expansion, instead of distraction.

. . . .

Dad,

You seem a long way away. When you don't see someone for a while, it seems like they only exist in memory and past. You can't remember if they're real or just someone you once saw in the late late movie some Friday night.

School continues, but it becomes more and more of an effort as time flows on. It can be a very unreal movie at times, you know. It's hard too, sometimes, because what I need to learn isn't always what my professor teaches or tests on. So I have to work twice as hard, reading between the lines for myself, and memorizing numbers and definitions for my grade.

It's a beautiful day here; it snowed again this morning. Not much, but I like the feelings it stimulates in me. The close, glossy gloom is quite a change from the scorching Indian days of the fall.

Life goes on very quietly. I tended to blow away a bit when I first came and tried to assimilate myself here, lots and lots of tension. But I'm over the hump and always do my best. A simple, subtle life alone is the best remedy for things like this, so I've just been doing a lot of weaving and drawing and reading and cooking and thinking and hiking and swimming. Since Ned left, I'm living alone, and am in no hurry to find a roommate. Occasionally I have some folks over for dinner, or go to a concert (I saw the symphony last week). But generally I sit at home or out in the woods somewhere. I guess getting your shit together is a full-time job. Sometimes I feel I neglect my human brothers too much, though. But I have a very hard time relating to most folks around me, at these times when my head breaks its leash and takes off—so I just try not to resist it.

One of my biggest frustrations is my frigidity when confronted with a group of people, or maybe just one. I sit in a class and completely schiz out, or I just freeze up; my brain won't think, and I spend my time striving for invisibility. I am incapable of presenting myself to strangers. Why am I so afraid of people, Dad? Is it because I just can't believe in myself? Or some type of social claustrophobia? I'm very tired of hiding. I wish I were a rock.

This is embarrassing, sitting in the student union with tears streaming down my face. It makes me so sad to see the people around me being happy all the time, living lives with purpose and direction and clarity. I feel like they swept the floors of the people factory and pasted the leftovers together to make me; introducing "the human collage."

Every day I feel I've lost more ground. I wake up every morning with a cold hollow moan. Someday I might wake up and find I can't speak or hear or see. I guess I've been cornered by myself, and I can't fight back. I either crouch down on the floor and hide my face, or try desperately to climb the walls. Life is no fun.

Shit,
Paul

So, along with the excitement and stimulation of a fresh start in a new locale, Paul was also sensing, from time to time, some of the fear and despair he carried within him.

Keeping a journal helped Paul enhance his gifts of insight and expression and, most importantly, focus on his search for rightness within himself. For the most part, this was private musing, though Paul shared

some of his journal writing with an art professor he admired. He contin-
ued his journals for the rest of his life, for which I am everlastingly
grateful.

College was a new challenge and a source of some reward for Paul,
but it did not succeed in yielding lasting satisfaction or meaning for him.
He grew restless and was in and out of school numerous times—starting
and quitting several jobs.

It also resulted in a case of the wanderlust, and the several excur-
sions of this period produced an interesting travelogue.

It was a week or so before my twentieth birthday. I'd just finished my first year of school. Nothing had really seemed to make
much sense. Nothing was even weird enough to make nonsense. I was
feeling pretty typical, petty, docile. Tired of words. Pages of them,
books of them, whole libraries full of them.

I was sitting down on Main Street watching the people roll by,
tourists and Texans and all that. And I thought of what some of my
friends were doing that summer. Building cardboard boxes or shaving
poodles or maybe even being the Head Pickler at Burger King. Shit, I
got pretty angry thinking of all this fresh young energy being wasted.
Folks just getting stiffer and staler every day. And then I got scared,
cause there I was sitting on that bench downtown no different than
anyone else, not being much or feeling much but frustration.

It seemed a little shock therapy might be in order. I decided what
I'd do is to put myself in as different and bizarre a situation as I could
find, and that I thought I could handle.

I went down to the library and played with the globe a while,
looked through some picture books, and flipped a few coins. And
then I marched on down and blew nearly all my savings on a ticket to
San Jose, Costa Rica. I figured maybe it'd be nice to take myself
someplace for my birthday.

I spent the next few days cleaning my house and packing up my
stuff, not thinking too much about what was coming up, but getting
pretty excited anyway.

I made myself a sign to hitch-hike with, and I went down by the bus station and stuck out my thumb. A few days and many weird Texas miles later I found myself in New Orleans, the afternoon of my birthday. There was a flight leaving that night, so I sat in the airport and let people buy me drinks and tell me beautiful and also horrible stories of far-off tropical paradises. Just before the plane leaves I decide I really ought to let my folks know where I'm gonna be, or where I wasn't gonna be. That was sure an interesting phone call.

Well, soon, here I sit on this airplane. It's my birthday and I'm kinda drunk and feeling real cocky, just lying back and daydreaming about Caribbean beaches, pineapples, and brown-skinned women.

We fly over the gulf, and make a stop in Guatemala. Here the American stewardesses and pilots get off and Latin Americans take their places. And some of the proud boisterous passengers get off and some smaller, meeker, darker ones take their places. We take off and fly for an hour or so, and then we stop in Nicaragua. I look at this little tiny airport out in the jungle, with tin buildings and a single, cracked and weed-covered runway. A few more Indians get on, and after a while I notice that none of the conversations are in English. And I start wondering about what I'm doing.

We pull into the Costa Rican airport a little before midnight. I'm staggering a bit as I get off the plane, maybe shaking a bit too. I walk up to the customs agent in my blue jeans and tennis shoes and my backpack. He looks at me and then at my passport, asks me what I'm doing (I don't really know), asks me where I'm going (haven't the faintest idea). He says something to his partner in Spanish that must've been pretty funny, he was laughing hard, then he looks straight at me and says, no, we cannot let you into our country. You'll have to leave.

What? What do you mean you can't *let* me in your. . . on and on and on. I start yelling and stamping my feet and causing quite a scene, much to everyone else's amusement.

So this guy takes me into his office and gets real frank about what he thinks and what he'd really like to do to me. So I had no choice but to turn around and walk out the door and back onto that plane, somehow thinking it was going to head back to the States.

Well, it didn't quite work out like that. An hour later I find myself in Panama, trying to get through their customs. I didn't want to be in Panama, but I showed them my money and I guess they really liked that cause they let me sign all their forms and they gave me a few shots and let me through.

It's about 2:00 in the morning now. I'm feeling pretty shell shocked, so I step on outside. The airport is all closed down and what I soon find out is that it sits in the middle of the National Militia Base, way out in the jungle. It's real dark, except for the lights in the watch towers and an occasional jeep, and the glow of cigarettes gleaming off the dark faces and polished guns of the soldiers walking up and down the road. And off in the distance I see one tiny cluster of lights. So I strap on my pack and just wade right on out into all this incredible reality.

In Panama City, Paul was able to arrange for a visa for Costa Rica, so he took a bus back to San Jose.

Padre,

I suppose about now you are on your way to work. That setting seems to be part of only a hazy dream, it's so far back in my past now. I guess that's how my memory works. And to think of all the time you've spent there over the years, how many thousands of days you've awakened to the dismal thought of its walls. I admire your constitution in the face of such an overwhelming burden, and your ability to grow under such odds as the city and its life.

I sit here at the Hotel Astoria, a small boarding house type establishment catering to young wanderers like me from all over the world. It's a small oasis in the middle of this strange city, San Jose, Costa Rica. A place to come in off the streets; a chance to speak English and talk of familiar things and places, and to exchange ideas on where to go and what to do and not to do. I wonder if you can picture it; I wish I were telepathic, I'd send you an image of it. I'm sure you'd find it interesting.

I wonder at my reasoning in coming here. Is it to recluse, hideaway, dodge my responsibility—or am I searching? I felt it might be good to get away from the things which help make Paul not Paul. In

Central America you can either completely isolate yourself, or else you must absolutely dedicate yourself and absorb into the culture. I'm not sure what I'm doing.

I'm learning many things, I guess, though. But I'm becoming very disappointed by what I've learned. I've discovered, contrary to what I've always thought, that I'm a very naive person, almost stupid at times. I'm terribly easily discouraged by anything, I have almost no ability to handle stress or to make decisions, and as is obvious, I have no faith whatsoever in myself. I never seem to directly experience anything, except in afterthought.

I'm really beginning to scare myself, Dad. I seem to have no direction whatsoever. I cannot hold a train of thought. I have no control at all over myself. I am either terribly depressed, or anxious, or confused. I hardly ever have an appetite; I hardly ever feel any satisfaction at all about something I've done. I feel like I'm wasting my life, and I feel like I'm wasting away, and I really have no idea what to do. I'm afraid because I'm twenty years old, and I have no idea what I'm about, what I've accomplished, what I can do, what I believe. I feel at the mercy of the wind and world. I don't want to end up a bum, or a lunatic, or just a listless wanderer. Some answers must arise.

I wish you and I could get along. Every day I find another similarity between us somehow. I really think an awful lot of you; it hurts me to see you hurt.

I don't know how long I shall be here; I haven't much money, and many things can happen. I feel the need to be an educated person, though. I really would like to find a school that could interest me and challenge me and tolerate me too. Do me a favor. Keep your eyes and ears open for such an opportunity, and for a job too; I may have to work for a while when I return. But I'm pretty sure I will be back in school in the fall, or winter for sure. I'll let you know more later. I feel a bit flaky today, so I think I'll catch a train for the coast.

Happy Birthday,
Pablito

. . . .

15

Saturday afternoon, the last weekend in June. I find myself in Cahuita, a small isolated settlement of blacks on the eastern coast of Costa Rica. The sky is heavy with clouds as the daily deluge works itself up into a fury. Walking out of town on the main road (the only road in a town so small you always seem to be walking out of town). It narrows to a pair of ruts not much more than a row of mudholes, and I follow this to the end, to a small hut nestled in the cocoa palms, with a yard full of chickens and small dogs, and a decrepit weathered shack that should have been abandoned years ago. All is quiet except for the clucking of the chickens and the roar of the surf as it breaks just a few yards offshore. On the front porch of the shack, facing out toward the sea, I find a young man swinging listlessly in an old tattered hammock, gazing, unseeing, out into the horizon where the grey of the sky kisses the pale blue sea. What entrancing scene is dancing now before the imaginative thoughts in the youthful mind's eye?

I'm freewheeling, that's right: found my way to the beautiful beaches of the Caribbean Sea. Here in Cahuita pretty much where I'd set my sights to come.

· · · · · · ·

So here I am on the beach with jungles and monkeys and palm trees and that beautiful sea breeze, and I just can't find my center. I am beginning to see how truly restless I am. I can't do any yoga and certainly not meditate; I've been getting high because it calms me down a bit, but I can't seem to stop giving myself such a hard time. Yet I am learning many things about myself that I wasn't aware of. How naive and meek I really am, how easily discouraged I become, how much more confused I am than I thought. I have been thinking much about motivation, and if it is right to just kick back and let things happen, and let it go at that. Is there such a thing as free will, and should I be taking control and exerting a bit of effort and trying to set my sights in some direction? It seems I have done little with my life but grow older, and that makes me very sad. I feel like I'm wasting my opportunity, and that time is running out, and I must set things right now, while I realize they are wrong—before I grow weary of trying and just let go to my stupidity.

16

. . . .

Many confusing feelings in the short time I've been here, and it sometimes makes me yearn for a companion—someone with patience for the vague ideas of youth, which often seem quite childish. At least to me, most of the profound and mystical revelations I've ever had can seem so trivial and obvious in hindsight. And I'm realizing I am a great one for realizing my mistakes from the front backwards. Which also means that I learn things the hard way, always putting more effort into something than is necessary, because I seem to scatter my energies over a large area of possibilities. I cannot pinpoint one direction to concentrate on. I am twenty years old and I have no idea where my path lies. And every time I seem to make some definite decision, and my life seems to solidify a bit, something unexpected comes up and blows my walls down; I am always starting all over again.

Reading back over this I find I'm not really expressing this right at all. At any rate though, I am very afraid. I came to Costa Rica because I felt stuck, and restless, and I felt the need to search for my next move; I am always either searching or waiting for my magical moment, a guru or something to instantly bring some peace and direction to my soul. I thought maybe if I got away from my usual setting, I might be able to calm down and to learn some helpful things and light some glowing candles to brighten my way. And some very outstanding things seem to have come to light, yet they're all very negative. My weaknesses are really becoming apparent.

I'm beginning to wonder if it was a mistake to come here at all, so I am leaving for Guatemala tomorrow, and if nothing works out there I shall have to admit defeat and return.

I have a future coming up to think about, and I want to make the most of it.

About eight months later, either due to more restlessness, or a sense of adventure, or just a desire for more variety, he found himself in Hawaii. It proved a beautiful experience.

Early morning at the sea, Pacific Ocean, Kauai. The sea in all its restless, hypnotic splendor. The ultimate indefinable rhythm of its waves, rising and falling endlessly without the extremes of lull or crescendo, expressing the emotion of the always almost, searching relentlessly, waiting for climax. Nothing sings so pure as this quicksilver sea.

The sun breaks loose from its cloudy eclipse, and the world is suddenly transformed into brilliant, warm Technicolor.

Little birds wade in the foam at the edge of the sand and the very great sea. Pelicans drop from the sky, and without hesitation, dive deep into the water. Farther out, in the crests of the larger waves, the dolphins swim along the shore, like opaque thoughts in the translucent mind of the sea. And even farther out are the whales. A solemn steady line of nomads heading south. Searching for spaces with room enough to loose their massive feelings.

I wade out into the water. In close the waves are playful, running up the beach, touching the shore, and with little cries of delight running back. But farther out, even at waist level, it is strong—the undertow pulling at my feet as the open sea sucks in its breath, and on the surface, the unpredictable waves surging up out of nowhere and rolling forward in an ever-growing wall of water. The power of the sea is terrifying.

I strap on my fins and mask and fight my way through the waves, riding up over the tops of the early ones, diving in primitive panic beneath the aggressive ones . Once out in calm deeper seas I can relax. I roll over on my back and drift gently on the swells, taking one last look at the sun and sky before I enter the foreign realm of the ocean. It presents a strange paradox, for deep inside I can feel its pull. I am moved by innate memories of primordial freedom and fulfillment in the sea. But I know that I no longer belong. My lungs don't work. Every movement is resistance, a clumsy attempt to overcome, for a few brief hours, the physical limitations of my humanity, so that I may experience the overwhelming beauty of the sea.

When I think of an edge, this is it. The surface of the sea is a separation of two worlds. Underwater, looking up, the bottoms of the waves are the sky, and the world exists below. It is a world of intense vividness. Sound is precise. Colors are pure. Physical sensation is a finely tuned experience.

Whenever I am in the water like this, it *visually* transmits its images *audibly* into my brain. What I see is heard almost as a symphony in my head. For the patterns of color and the patterns of motion and movement, the winds of the sea and its creatures are incredibly tied to a universal rhythm, and nothing is done out of key or off tempo. A school of thousands of tiny fish moves in such synchronicity as to appear as a single organism. Forests of kelp sway back and forth in unison. Giant fish swim stoically along like princes or wizards. There are no secrets here. Everything knows itself.

The sea is all captivating. It takes my thoughts and my mind. There is no need for reason. I can forget myself for hours. By giving myself up to the sea, I can know what it feels like to cease to exist.

. . . .

Hello—

Well Padre, some more notes from far distant lands to spice up your day, and give you something new to wonder at. Here lies your son in a park in Wiamea on the south shore of Kauai, garden paradise of the world, it seems. The sun is about to set in the sea, just a short leap away. Andy and I, and his guitar of course, lie here moaning and groaning, weak and feverish from drinking some bad water, I guess. It gives me a chance to think of and write to my always-neglected father, though.

It sure is strange how the wanderlust can strike and carry me far from my home and friends and things I know so well. I feel that maybe my erraticness and indecision scares you sometimes. It scares me, for sure.

Thanks for your recent help when I needed it. I should never write to you on these tiny postcards; I'll send a real letter off later. Until then, have faith in this silly hobo. It helps.

Paul

. . . .

Early morning sounds, so soft and soothing, whisper in my ears, and pull me gently from my dreams. High on a grassy cliff I awake, and a breeze blows quiet thoughts through my hair. A young goat bleats its youthful hunger, morning glories rise and take their first deep breaths. On the rocks below the waves crash in like the frenzied faces of a thousand ancient men, powered by the anger of anyone who has ever died. Yet farther out to sea thirty-foot waves meet and merge as gently as a kiss. Beyond, the wind, prince of the earth, leads an army of clouds marching to the far reaches of the horizon, and magically disappears in the razor's edge of sky and sea. Today, my life is as a poem. Yet soon again I will wonder and doubt, and the clouds will blow down from the mountains.

. . . .

Well, California again, cold and windy and frustrating. It seems to make Hawaii that much more real. After Andy returned to the forty-eight, I went back to Poipu and hid out in the trees for a while. I realize I've been trying to grow up too soon. I gotta be patient. I found a lot more strength inside of myself. And I found a great need to create, though I don't know where it'll take me, or what tools I'll choose to express with. That will take some time.

I see now how important it is to get out of myself, in order to learn of myself, and my means to that end is through other folks. "What proof have I of my own existence save other people's reaction to me." Everything I see is a reflection of myself; it is good to be with people different than me, to see the things I am not, and to identify the things I am.

Damn, I've got so many almost thoughts; I can see them out of the corner of my mind. I sure have a bunch of work to do; it feels good. I hope I never tire, or get too scared to keep searching.

DISORDERED ECSTASY

The Twenty-second Year

Now I sit here again in Durango, in a spot I've recently found, close to the river, close to some trees, with shade and with sky and horizon in silhouette too. Just one place close to home, like the hundred other exquisitely striking places I pass by every day on my travels. Yet somehow different. Somehow here like a center of quiet, the eye of a storm where I can go and not be seen. Where calmness and the joy of being seem to pervade the air like sunrays. Where, like now, if I choose, it can be silent and softly-lit dusk for as long as I need it to be. Until these fragments of thoughts, drifting inside and into my head like a mass of entropic dust, gather together in one straining, yet complete, idea run its course, and I can take the imprint of this and fit one more piece into this giant puzzle that is me.

. . . .

I want so hard to be at peace. And I want so much to be able to listen to my heart—to follow where it leads. And to reach out to people—to draw people toward me instead of scaring them off. I need to find some direction, to base my life on something. I want to laugh, and to cry, and be glad, and be ready to die.

. . . .

Dear Chuckles,

I've always wanted to call you that. It would make a beautiful nickname for someone, although it's hardly something to call your father. It sure brings up a lot of emotions to think of you. At weaker moments I tenderly file you away for another day. I sure wish we were more at peace with each other, and with ourselves; it sure ain't from lack of trying.

Going to paradise and back did some things to my head—like bringing the weight of responsibility down on it. I realize I'm too lazy to be a realist, and too much of a coward to be an idealist. It always feels like my gears are turning—they just won't engage. I'm a very almost person, I guess. I'm always afraid to change, but I know it's what I have to do. I don't want to grow up too quickly, yet that's what the world expects of me. I want very much to finish school, but I don't know why, so I guess it should wait.

I was hurt that you didn't want to help me with my inlaid bread-board project; a few years ago you would've jumped at the chance. I'm out of bucks and was thinking if I could do a real fine job on this, I could maybe start making and selling them on consignment, or get backed by someone and buy my own tools so I could really get started, and perhaps make my money on things that would bring some joy. It all seems like a wet dream now. I don't want you to feel bad; I just want you to know how I feel. I'm still gonna try anyhow.

I finally got a story published in a local magazine; that made me feel kinda proud.

I hope things go well with you; we're almost one and the same, and when you hurt, it hurts me too.

Sorry you have to read so much between the lines, I still haven't gotten over being afraid of you I guess. You are very special to me.

Paulo

Dear Paul,

I, too, agonize over our sometimes persisting pain and lack of peace with each other. I'm glad it doesn't come up any more often than it does, and I have a lot of optimism that our relationship will continue to get better—as I feel it has now for several years. Sometimes I find myself wishing we lived together again; other times, that doesn't seem like it would work.

Part of what comes out of me right now, I would guess, reflects what I'm going through relative to my near future. As you know, I'm within maybe less than a year of getting all the necessary details accommodated to pull off the most drastic change in my life—in moving away from a twenty-five-year-long career, away from the city, out into the seclusion and strangeness of the forest, to start over. Intense.

At this point, I don't have any remaining doubt of its being right for me. I am nearly overwhelmed, however, by the magnitude and diversity of things to take care of, carefully, so that it works—so that it accomplishes what I want it to, and doesn't bring on new problems so massive that I can't find ways to handle them. I hope that my foresight is really adequate for this.

Don't misunderstand: it's still quite exciting, and I'm not going to change my mind about it. But I have to admit that it's also scary, from time to time. One of the advantages of this move is that you and I will be only fifty miles apart, for a while, at least. That feels great.

Stay well, and know that I love you deeply, and want the very best for you. It's deserved.

Thoughtfully,
Dad

Summer time and being young sure go together well—vitality and lust and adventure. I had a little fling for a week with a girl named Annette, a friend of a friend. With big bright eyes that look right through you. A rich California girl who liked to draw and play music and sing—to laugh, to give, to be alone. She brought home lots of flowers, bought me a big bottle of Drambuie, and started crying, like only a woman can, one night as we made love.

I showed her the mountains, and she showed me *me* once again. I found out what a nice guy I really can be. It sure felt good to make someone else feel good. And it sure doesn't feel right being alone anymore. A week is just long enough to keep it light, but to get real close too.

She was a beautiful person, vague yet honest as a child, and I hope I haven't seen the last of her.

· · · · · · ·

I've been thinking about the conflict that arises between a person's social concern and his own personal responsibility. And it seemed to me, when I've dug down deep, emptied out all the pockets of my personal experience and dumped it out in front of me, lint and all, that we really have no social consciousness. But that, quite simply, the only way we can act is to become as good a friend to ourself as we can. If we can learn, through practiced calmness and faith, to dip our buckets of need deep into that quiet, fathomless well of our being, we will always draw back a full load of answers. And for me it will always be different, in some way, than for someone else. And for me to try to live by their values, for me to act out my play with their script would be madness.

A person can only prepare himself for a crisis or decision by freeing himself from everything but his self. And if rational action is called for, by using only as his tools those few thoughts or memories of experience that have truly touched him.

We will never be confronted by a reality beyond our cumulative experience.

· · · · · · ·

I need to say now, and keep reminding myself, that I am a searcher. Above all, I want a rich and fulfilling life; I want to dwell in life's mysteries; I want to be different than most people.

I was extremely busy with preparations to conclude a career managing a corporation engaged in scientific research and begin a new, and simpler, lifestyle in the country. Meanwhile, Paul again succumbed to the wanderlust. His next trip was a leisurely one through the Southwest and California.

After two years of college, followed by a summer of little but work, stress, empty relationships, and just a general gangrene of the spirit, I decide to go a-questing, as they say. Winter is coming on strong—too strong—so I think it might be best to maybe leave it behind, try to leave as much as possible of me and my images behind too, quit struggling so much. Maybe by seeking out the sunshine, steeping myself in the easy life for a while, simply opening up and letting new winds blow through me, that some things might just figure themselves out—if only given the freedom to do so. So once again I pack everything up, stash it all away. I buy an old VW bus, with a bed and stove and stereo and sink and refrigerator, and enough room for a bicycle, a mandolin, and a few books—leave Colorado, and head for the California coastline, first going south.

· · · · · · ·

Waking in New Mexico, alone, uncertain and frightened. Wondering in awe at the changes in the world, now that there is only me. Cold. My mind befogged by the wispy reminders/remainders of dreams, telling me the elusive answers that I am chasing. On to Santa Fe.

Quiet now. Just the tree-wind-dance and a cocky crow. Camped at Black Forest Campground, Hyde Park. Lots of room in my bus: lots of room for possessions; lots of room for worry. Just another sliver working its way into my subconscious thoughts.

I'm beginning to see how you don't really *develop* creativity and freewheeling thought, you only remove all the things hiding it from view. Here I lie within my cozy little turtleshell, parked alongside a quiet moonlit road, incense burning, candles flickering, snuggled into blankets, a full belly glowing from within. Nowhere to be; nothing need be done. Just waiting to see. Just me.

· · · · · · ·

The heart, the very center of the painted desert; petrified forests lie passively on the fringes, a prehistoric Pompeii. Lying naked on the moonscape bed of a giant arroyo, crumbly like a piece of burnt toast— so dry you don't worry about water, you worry about air. Faded colors in need of a shine; the borderline of life, a thin spot in the grand illusion of planet earth, almost transparent. Stinking of an hereditary memory, midway in the course of life's awakening.

I left Santa Fe last night; during my shower I sensed a dozen subtle signs that things were right. Made some good solid friends, left no regrets or doubt—just another new experience to slowly digest and quietly metabolize into my self.

I can see that, beneath my seemingly surface shallowness, that beneath the ice the river still flows; in spite of my preoccupation and inattentive attitude and worry, I am picking up on many things that are happening around and inside of me. For at times these insights and truths come spontaneously to mind without any thought or effort at all.

· · · · · · ·

Oak Creek Canyon: my favorite spot in Arizona—rock much like the Animas Valley north of Durango, rosy Hermosa sandstone topped by another layer of a milky-hue. Waking in an early morning paradise at an overlook point near the head of the canyon. Looking down into a shadowy pit, a giant bird sanctuary, with tiny dots of sunlight dancing through the air, reflections on satiny wings as they flash and dive across the sky below.

Then, hiking up a thin, tall, tall canyon, a Sunday-strolling trail along a green-pine, thickly-oaked, orange and red forest: footsteps echoing off the walls, a solemn, deep and virtuous creek washing down the middle. A canyon slit, giant crevasse gouging back forever in a narrow desert Eden below the surface of the earth.

· · · · · · ·

California now. Calmness on the shore at Moonlight Beach; dolphins in the crest of waves. Staying in the barn-sanctuary-temple of good friends (and good medicine), Andy and Sarah. Being with them revives all my faith in the power of love, justice, good will and thoughts; in man's ability, my ability, the beauty of living.

Free time by the sea, health, friends, being, hoping, trying; it sure feels good, taking some responsibility for my life.

· · · · · · ·

Leaving friends now. Losing laughter and light-hearted smiles to my never-ceasing restlessness, and hurting bad. Trying to find that balance between feeling and clinging, washing my pain away or drowning in it.

Yet knowing I have the strength to overcome my panic and my fear. Hoping I can become clearer, *solider* through all the aloneness—instead of *harder*. Wondering if I've put myself in some type of terrible exile too, in not knowing why I drift and drift like this. Hoping my pain and my incomprehensible sorrow are really necessary.

. . . .

Ralph's house. Getting ready to head out once again, after the luxury of friendship and a warm home. Restless, yet not wanting to rush, but still feeling somehow I should be moving on. Wondering what I'm doing, why I've taken this journey—or if it's taken me? Maybe wanting to see new places, old friends—compare my home and myself against others' development.

Perhaps I just left to leave, though, trying to outrun myself. But it seems to be working a bit; I've calmed down, occasionally looking to see if, for my near future, I want work, school, or travel.

I guess for now I just keep moving north. I'll find a place to camp a while, check out the scene, the occupants, the feel, the opportunities. Try to go slowly, deliberately, watch myself; I've got some strength now. Maybe hope that in my indecision and laziness, something will come my way, and that I'll be aware enough to see it, jump on it. If not, I guess I'll just be a scared, broke, homeless wanderer. Write a lot, pick, draw, talk to folks, watch, eat right, don't drink, be calm, be thrifty, hope.

. . . .

Now, I sit in here, crouched in a blackened hollow redwood tree, rain drizzling down in driplets that strike the ground with a crackle. Immense fluted columns rising up and through a warm sky of fog. Luminous light seeping down to the ground. Be like a tree; just be rained on. These guys are digging it in a wise and meditative way, fitting to their size and age. Ecstatic gods. My damp petty thoughts must surely be an itchy irritant to their gentle knowings. So I think softly.

. . . .

It is getting to be pretty late; I'm almost to the northern edge of the Big Sur coastline, so I pull off onto a little turnaround that lies between the sea and Highway One—a few yards below the level of the pavement. I lay my sleeping bag out on the ground so that I can be with the moon and stars, and the sound of the waves. Just before daylight a terrific storm starts brewing. The wind begins blowing and howling fiercely, and huge masses of black clouds sweep in from over the sea.

I crawl into my bus and try to go back to sleep, but it is pitching back and forth so violently in the wind that I decide I'd better move on down the road and try to find someplace with more shelter. I'm stretched out in back pulling on my pants when I hear a terrible noise of screeching tires, tearing metal and breaking glass. Turning to look out the curtains (which are closed to block out headlights) toward the highway, I see a huge shadow descending on my bus. I jump forward just at impact, amidst a shower of glass and a terrible crash. Looking out the seaside windows, I see another VW bus roll down the hill two or three times, and come to a stop on its bottom a little way away, just a mass of mangled metal. The first I see is a high chair lying on the ground.

I don't feel good about how I reacted. I was scared to go check the other person out, but luckily there were already other people on the scene. And I was more concerned about my poor bashed-in bus than about the other driver, a girl. Shitty attitude. I cried a bit later, and have been rather shaky and unsteady since. Now I'm just waiting to figure out the insurance and all.

Later in the evening, after a very intense day, I'm sitting in a small, warm coffeehouse feeling very fragile and alone, drinking warm liqueurs and working on a drawing to send to my sister for her birthday.

A striking young lady walks in. She has red hair (my greatest weakness), a simple lavender dress like a peasant gown, and an old guitar dangling caseless down her back, banging off the door and tables as she walks by.

She comes by, very amiably, admires my work, smiles, and then sits down in the corner with a man who is obviously acquainted with her. After a while she begins to play her guitar and to sing softly.

There are few people inside, just me and this girl, her friend, and an older couple. But the waitress goes over and says I'm sorry, you can't sit in here and play that thing, we haven't got a license for it, or something equally ridiculous.

The restaurant sits on the garden level of a group of shops clustered out a tiled courtyard, with some palm trees and tables and a huge iron cauldron with a large fire going in it. Since it's a Sunday night none of the shops are open, except the coffeehouse. So nobody is around except maybe an occasional couple strolling around window shopping, maybe arguing, maybe just being in love. Carmel attracts a lot of wealthy foreign second-honeymooners.

The redhead and her friend decide to sit out in the courtyard and pick and sing, and she asks me and this other couple if we'd like to join them. So it's kinda chilly out, I sit by this fire and sip on hot drinks and listen to this lady sing old love songs and gentle ballads in this lovely, soft voice.

One of these couples strolls by, stops in the shadows and listens for a while. The girl finishes her song and asks them to join us. And they sit down real shyly. She asks them where they're from, and maybe they say Belgium. So she starts singing some exquisite Belgian love song, in Belgian. You should see these folks' faces light up! They move in a little closer and take off their shoes and order everyone a drink, and sit and listen.

Another couple walks up, and perhaps they're Hungarian. So this girl strums her guitar and sings a rousing Hungarian dance. And these folks start clapping their hands and then they get up and start dancing and jumping all around. And soon here are some Frenchmen, seeing what all the commotion is, and for them she sings a French lullaby, and they start thinking of home and get all soft and glassy-eyed.

This just went on for hours, and this girl never missed a song; she knew songs in over forty languages. In fact, she was writing a doctoral thesis on folk music, and had just finished a world tour.

By the end of the night there were several dozen people gathered together. People from all over the world, who would rarely venture even a smile at one another. And here we all were dancing and singing and crying and laughing and hugging and just getting totally carried away. This went on until we were exhausted. And everybody left with a smile, looking so much younger, lighter. It was one of the finest lessons I've ever had. A truly rare experience.

· · · · · · ·

Point Lobos Preserve. Sitting in the sun on a crusty rock, with birds and croaking silly sea lions, and a restless sea. Jewels of tiny tide pools and an ugly family of pelicans all in a line. Leaving Carmel today. I like it better than anywhere else, so far. Its tiny exquisite shops, narrow streets and quiet hidden homes and inns. The inns are so beautiful—tucked-away old buildings where one could surely lose oneself in another time.

· · · · · · ·

Quiet easy days. A lesson in the spirit of the Tao. How to be. Trying to find a balance between the beauty and the pain. You just can't open up all at once.

The ocean today is the finest I've seen it—the sky just a paleness, with darker wind-sculpted cumulus radiating from the sun—the water very constant, rhythmic.

It rained last night, a beautiful seaside rain. Feeling the air and the sky become fuller and fuller, and finally the rain meeting the sea and exploding in a burst of orgasm, and continuing to fall gently, soothingly, all night. And today it's like the world has cleared out, not wanting to distract the earth in the joy of its long-awaited succulent moisture.

· · · · · · ·

Well, back in Colorado now, sitting on a rock near Baker's Bridge, so quiet after a few frenzied days of last-minute overload. People here seem so blue, uncertain and fragile. I'm so affected by it. Me, I feel like ninety-weight oil flows through my veins: hard to move, to try to work it all out. It sure has been good to be with the folks here, though; faces all over that I know. But none seem too happy. So it's still me, only and just. Where to now; what for; how?

· · · · · · ·

Though it seems at times that things don't always work out right, and that I have no goals or direction, that I wander lost, I think I always know that I have the sincerity and the energy, the determination and devotion to excel, when I find what is looking for me. And until that time occurs, take it as it comes—to the max; be honest and above all be good to other people, and to yourself. Love and faith is gonna get me through. And someday I'll be able to look at myself with pride.

· · · · · · ·

Glad to be back among good friends, familiar scenes surrounding me in this setting almost like a vicarious womb. Yet feeling twinges of guilt at being here too, where I've already been. It seems a bit like a scene from "I Never Promised You A Rose Garden" where a patient going out is almost knighted, a saint to inspire all aspiring hearts, yet always he returns, lost and overwhelmed, to the comfort and the laziness of craziness.

But then again, there's an old saying: "Blossom where you're planted" that is beginning to make sense to me now. As much as I enjoy traveling, and as much as I hoped to find new directions and a new start somewhere else, at times I feel defeated at having returned empty-handed, no new gospel for the folks back home. But, besides all that, I feel a certain calm at being here, pretty much backed into a corner without a job, without money, without any revelations. My trip to California sure showed me where the work lies. But, it scares me witless to think of the task of changing myself, of breaking the bonds of the patterns of habitual thought and needless worry that have formed such a solid foundation in my being—yet which I know to be so detrimental and, in a way, almost evil. I have so much work to do on myself before I can ever look at myself with any kind of pride. But having made that decision I guess I am really committed. I know now that ignorance is bliss!

I returned to Durango with this rationale: what it feels like I want to do now is to enroll in a school overseas, somewhere in Europe—to combine my ways of wander with some degree of responsibility. So I'll need a base, to refurbish my finances, to check out the various programs available, to get my act together so to speak. It seemed that Durango would be the best place to do this; my closest contacts are here, friends, references, etc. But so far nothing has come together. I find myself with a need for some responsibility, something to test myself with, something which would require a summoning of my resources.

So far I find myself unable to make any use out of what I've learned in the past twenty-one years. And what I need to concentrate on now is a little output, something to show for all this time I've spent watching and listening. I hope I'll always be looking for those out-of-the-ordinary opportunities.

· · · · · · ·

I have these times, say on an evening ride north up into the valley, when the last bright sunlight is shining over the valley floor. The trees, grasses, and river are absolutely saturated with light after a full day of brilliant sun. The high country is sucking in its breath, and the wind is a steady exhilarating broom sweeping through my senses. My bicycle is singing down the road.

A change comes over me like some kind of rare chemical reaction inside. The world shifts into a powerful crystalline state. Distinctly alive, yet dreamy, like a journey into a water-colour book.

As hard as I've ever tried, I have never been able to deliberately incite this perception. Its appearance is always a great surprise, sometimes so overwhelmingly captivating that I don't even notice the transition. But I am always so awed at the source of power it might become, if one could tap into such a state of being with some type of coherent direction or purpose in mind.

Anything could happen.

. . . .

There's a place that I will sometimes have access to that spontaneously wells up out of my deepest imagination. Sometimes it occurs as a dream. Sometimes it appears at those times of raw intensity when I let myself go and ride the crazy waves of reality, instead of flailing around and trying to drown myself in panic. It almost seems to be a type of womb image. Or, maybe, of the tomb—projecting myself into the place beyond all ends. It occurs to me as a complete, deliberate sensual experience, yet involving and affecting more than just the five senses. I guess for anything in our unconscious mind—an idea, feeling, or essence—to be perceived by our conscious, it must take on physically symbolic form.

It is a land in waiting, without time or movement. Only when I appear as a man is there any indication of change. I have often felt this when I was deep in the woods alone. Until I had come, the forest was like an intricate, silent, immobile stage set, and only my presence made the wind blow, the rain fall, the birds cry.

It is a land of soft contrast, like a painting by Turner or Pissarro. The colors merge and melt into each other like a mist, no two complementary colors occurring side by side. No sharp, distinct lines of horizon, contour or silhouette bisect the landscape. Even the birds are the same color as the sky they fly through.

It's hard to tell the difference between a sound and a smell, a sight or a thought. The spectrum of senses ceases to be a linear reception. So the landscape can be very melodic, the wind colorful, a birdsong soft to the skin, the rain, compassionate.

It is a place of disordered ecstasy. And if the transition from this state of mind to a normal state is too sudden, it can come as quite a shock. This world is too sharp, loud, crowded and confusing, and maybe a little bit too real.

. . . .

Springtime in Colorado. Early spring days of contrast: one moment it's grey, bleak, chills that seem to be the neurosis of Mother

Earth, and the next time you look out the window, the mud and slush have dissolved and heat waves are drifting above the streets in radiant sunshine.

It makes me feel like a yo-yo. I'll just have about resigned myself to a day inside, after spending hours of terrible battle with the depressive gloom that envelopes the earth, inscaping down deep into the sanctuaries of mind, blissfully ignorant of the burdens of physical being—and suddenly the sun bursts out like a bright light, an alarm clock throwing a sleeper from fluid dreams into sudden consciousness, and I'll have to make that quick transition into solidity and movement. But I feel better that way. My vitalness and also my distraction are based on physical things.

The past few months I have found more people who I can be with and who can comfortably be with me (I seem to be growing up into a little more understanding of give and take) and it really helps a lot. But it also, by contrast, makes my loneliness much more painful, something I still have never learned how to cope with gracefully—to say the least. At twenty-one, life seems so incredibly intense and complex that I am truly suffering from a claustrophobia of being. And like a dancer thrown off balance, I lurch back and pitch forward in a panicky grab for rightness. I keep thinking that as I grow older and become more aware of what I'm about, that things will become calmer and clearer, simpler. But I guess my work has just begun and the hard part still lies ahead, cause everyday I feel more ignorant and naive and confused. So my real focus now is just to try and keep things light.

I am finding myself with many creative ideas and a stimulation of thought and feeling, but I've let the circumstances of my life get pretty run down and it's been taking all my energy to hold together and form all the particulars into some sort of a usable mass. So I spend my time trying to weigh out the worry with a generous share of beauty on the side.

. . . .

It seems that all of the concepts, morals, or ideas that I try to share are really just a part or a conglomerate of all I've ever read or been told. (Whatever the philosophy, no matter how complex or com-

34

plete it may be, it is merely a string of phrases or relative observations that I have somehow selected from my memory and lumped all together as a part of my personality.)

I have never felt as if I've really ever expressed something that was truly me, that was a valid communication of my own experience. I wonder at how much closer to myself I might be, had I never read a book or taken a class or watched TV?

I would like to believe that, as much as I feel that the ultimate and fundamental experience in life is to share, I would hope that I as a singular being, would have something totally unique to bring into this vast touching.

. . . .

Springtime has come with a sigh of relief and a childish lighthearted hopefulness. A time of soulful rest and healthy distraction— for building of one's creative strength.

At this time I made a pivotal move: leaving my career in the city, and acquiring an old homestead in the midst of the National Forest in southwest Colorado, my wife and I began a new life, just fifty-or-so miles from Paul's Durango setting.

This would involve building a new house, learning new skills, and upsetting my previous priorities totally; and it meant being able to live close enough to Paul to make possible much more frequent contact. It also allowed him to participate, from time to time, in many of the projects in my new life, resulting in rewarding times together.

I'm sitting here on the porch facing west off the rickety musty cabin sitting on my father's land, and soon-to-be new homesite. He asked me to spend a week or so here watching over the place and doing some preliminary work while he goes back to Denver to pack his belongings and wife and cat and move them down here for good.

It being springtime and already having had a month or more of youthful, lighthearted weather, I thought to use this opportunity to be alone, far away from the circumstances of men. To fast, and give my body a much needed rest and cleaning, and just spend my time walking through the woods, watching the springtime blossom and sprout and rush in little creeklets down the mountains. Be simple and calm and try to clear the ominous fog that has been growing above my head like some monstrous thundercloud.

But, alas, every day has been bitter winds and snow—yes snow— day after day, piling up all around the windows, and peering in like a crowd of ghosts. This little cabin has no heat, hot water, or fireplace, so I have spent most of my time wrapped up in warm blankets and quilts, sleeping and reading. Which is all the better, for I realize how I sorely needed the rest.

Rest has been good, and its gentleness soothing, and I've tried not to think of anything at all but pleasantness and pureness. Yet times come when I feel so lost and alone and I don't know whether to give in to these feelings and learn the lesson they have to offer, or whether I should fight and overcome those moments of weakness. It is a strange puzzle to me.

Luckily I brought several books with me, for it has even been too cold to pull out my mandolin.

My brief respite of sun and blue skies is almost over; here come the clouds once again. So I think I'll go lunch on my apple juice and then back into hibernation.

· · · · · · ·

A fine rainy day, just a steady enough mild gentle rain to be out in it a bit.

When searching for an image with which to express, it is essential for me to expose myself to as many external powers and stimulants as possible, in order to sort through my various feelings and beings as I react to these situations. I need to try to pinpoint the primary essence, idea, or emotion to be expressed; only then can I seek out its physical interpretation as it reacts with my personal experience.

The rain is not only a powerful stimulant, for me it is also peaceful and satisfying—whether from being cloaked in the womb of water in its purest form, or from some type of atmospheric reaction, or a fond memory-feeling, or perhaps the abandon of simply being quiet.

· · · · · · ·

Yeah. Today I complete my twenty-second revolution, and begin my twenty-third. So to acknowledge myself and to somewhat express to the world the essence of *my* spirit, I set out alone and undistracted on a short journey into the pure beauty of nature.

There is a sense in the wilderness that one is experiencing the ultimate in the spirit world, as well as the ultimate in physical expression. From walking through the deepest, greenest intricacy of the forest to climbing up to the top of the barest, most immense hunk of stone (with nothing in view except thoughts)—that is, in the purest sense, without the distraction of anything that is unreal. I can confront exactly where my own realities lie, if I so choose.

I want to be a person who can bring a smile to someone's face, who can always be trusted, even in unstable situations. Someone people come to for a little truth, and maybe adventure and lightheartedness too. But most of all truth and love, which may sound a little corny, but sure does work.

Romance in Durango
The Twenty-third Year

We speak of our goals, our designs, expectations, the pathway we are laying for ourselves. A doctor, an architect, an interior designer.

So I think about what concerns *me*; what affects *me* the most, excites or disturbs. And the answers that appear sometimes seem so abstract that they lose all practical application. I think that communication is my priority: inspiration, compassion, communion, expression. I want to become like a tuning fork, resonating empathetically with all with whom I come into contact. I am so tired, so unbalanced by the absence of human response to each other, the apathy and the fear, that just to make someone angry is a victory.

To experience those times when a real connection is made, when that surge of understanding is transmitted from another person into myself—to be touched in such a way will always be my incentive, my faith. So many people are trying to convince themselves, to convince me, that human nature is to repel and not attract. It is almost as if to find friendship or love is an accident, an exception to the rule.

But I cannot accept that. It is an unnatural reaction to feel fear or mistrust. It took me years of pain and humiliation to learn to disbelieve, to hide from the goodness of men. And it will take all those years again, plus some, to unlearn those traits, even though in my heart I know them as viscous habits.

That sensitivity is exactly what I wish to pursue, and what I wish to use as my vehicle through whatever comes my way. The rest will take care of itself.

. . . .

Someone spoke in class today of "the edge." I think a lot about those times. That chaotic gap, that empty hesitation we experience at times of change.

To me it is almost a basic emotion, something inherent that responds when we are exposed to an unknown or unexpected experience of the external world.

If I'd never experienced a fall or a spring, there would be no difference between my feelings toward the two. But I am a human, and I make all these correlations within—so the edge I feel at fall is also not the edge that someone else would feel. Just as the fear I feel (or the lust, or the joy) is very different from theirs. So there are really no universal emotions, no purity or essence of feeling. (Except maybe love. And love is like the color white; it is all colors.)

These periods of edge are an important time for me. They are one of my best tools. The edge is an emptiness—or better yet, an openness. It is the emotion of change. Many times this is expressed as dichotomy, as in the case of death. And then the edge is seen as a fine line dividing two poles.

But usually, in most of the situations where it is exposed, the edge is really just the awareness that you are at that place, that common ground, where you have the freedom to move or to view as you will it. And if you are prepared for this, if you can maintain your center and not be overcome by doubt, or by goals too long anticipated, or by any self-inflicted limitations, then this can be a moment of great potential power.

I was told once that success is when preparation meets opportunity. And then edge is just an acknowledgment that we have entered into a natural phase of opportunity.

. . . .

It is barely daybreak, the moon is cradled in the fork of a jade tree, silhouette in the window as I lie here in my bed, in this temple that is my bedroom. Even in the shallow moonlight and the tiny beam from a lamp, this room is very alive, responsive, affirmative. It is wall-to-wall and ceiling-to-floor plants, hanging or sitting or climbing along every available space, aglow with whatever light they can find.

The room is long and thin. The west wall is all windows, and a big glass door opening outside into the garden. I really like that door. On warm nights I can sit half in and half out and look into the sky, or watch the sun set behind Perins Peak. And sometimes in the night a person will slip in the back unbeknownst to the rest of the house, like a secret lover. The bed is brass—wide and low, tucked in the corner and piled high with pillows and soft, full blankets. Pictures and paintings of young girls and forests, weavings of deep rich colors adorn the walls nearby. It is a warm spot, a gentle world in which to wake every morning, easing into reality each day with images of beauty, and reminders of better ways.

Books are stacked everywhere—always within reach. Picture books, writing books, real books, ideal books, a book to stimulate or a book to chase away any mood or thought. Often before I sleep I will pick out a book and maybe look long at a painting by Monet or a passage by Jung or a photo from my past. And that will set the stage for my dreams.

And if I am sensitive to my needs at that time, that will be enough to trigger a change, and sometimes—far too seldom—I can wake up a new person, a little lighter, a little freer. I appreciate the nighttime and the power of sleep. Always, when working with an idea, searching for an image to project, struggling to express myself in form, I will take my half-done drawings and pin them to the wall where I can see them before I sleep or when I wake. Never to be studied, just being available is enough, for I find my best ideas from the corner of my eye.

It's important for me to keep this room tidy, to have everything available. The floor is clean, books are stacked, clothes are hung, the bed always gets made, shoes sit in a line in the closet.

But sometimes I'll look around, under the bed, in the corners, in spots unused and unseen, thick with dust and forgotten items stuffed away in a moment of haste. And it kinda scares me. Dust in the corners of my mind.

. . . .

Things for me lately have been rough. Rough with the pain of seeking and finding the unexpected answer. Knowledge too potent to practice in life, which throws me into an abyss of confusion. Torn by the gap of that human condition which enables one to see what he could be, and then what he really is.

Fear of crossing such distances, fear of letting go to the tides and winds and powers that lead and direct. Fighting the overwhelming. The painful breaking up of the subjective and objective. Guilty because of the love I take, and the uncertainty I reflect to the striving world around. Unwilling to change. Unable to be content.

Still, never losing that fascination for the whole, incomprehensible situation. Thinking seriously that there is really no wrong in pursuing and basing my own foundation of reality in a naively dreamlike approach to the world. Seeking and giving only of a simple beauty found in the quiet breeze of treetop thoughts. Seeing imagically all that affects me and my motivations toward it. I get too caught up in the responsibility of living, never realizing the joy of being or doing, as a prime incentive toward action and thought.

Been working lately for Dad, helping him on his house in the woods. Quiet, easy, yet intense working conditions—little pressure except that which I manifest, the luxurious tiredness that follows a day of hard work. Watching my father grow, calm down. Watching someone who has learned to listen to his heart, with a minimum of those agers: doubt and confusion.

Soon that will be over, though, and I have accepted a job in the restaurant I once worked in, but it is a tense, pressure-filled job, and I can't make a full commitment to it; I hate to feel my freedom slip away, though I make such poor use of it.

. . . .

I dreamed of being in an incredibly large house. Its walls were of rosewood and black marble. The ceiling was of carved ebony, the floors of Carrara marble covered with ancient elaborately hand-tied rugs. I stood on the third or fourth floor, looking down through a circular rotunda that exposed the floors below. A huge party or celebration was taking place. People were milling around, drinking and talking, admiring the astonishing collection of artwork which adorned the various rooms. An orchestra was playing and people danced passionately across an immense ballroom with stone floors and massive candelabras hanging from the roof. There is a dining room: a long crystalline room full of tables of chattering people, drinking toasts and feasting, laughing uproariously.

I feel vaguely out of place. I can't figure out why I'm there—why I'm dressed in this satin suit and congregating with these obviously extremely wealthy people. So I wander around a bit, creating this electric little space around me, acting very intent in my appraisal of the house, so people will keep their distance and not stop me to talk, asking me just what was my name and my business, what football team did I own, who was my hairdresser.

And I'm walking down the front hallway, thinking maybe I should slip out and head home, when I am confronted by this door, this absolutely exquisite hardwood door, massive—yet delicate. Hanging on hinges as smooth as clockwork. Inlaid with a scene—done in exotic hardwoods, metal and stone—of a young female warrior or goddess, sitting astride a huge peacock-swan, her head thrown back in exaltation, the bird just leaving the ground. There is a window of tinted beveled glass, etched into a kaleidoscope sun, with light refracting from its center. The doorknob is elaborately cast bronze, and is inlaid with stone in the shape of a Chinese star ⅄ which is my own personal watermark or symbol.

So I realize that it was *I* who made this superb door, and that this gala celebration was a dedication of the house and all its incredible workmanship. And that I was a part of this elite group which had collaborated on this house.

I awoke feeling very fulfilled. I would sure like to make that door someday.

· · · · · · ·

There has been an idea, an image, which I have been formulating in my mind the past few years. I have begun to realize the advantage of having some type of ideal or conscious image of myself which I can project myself into.

So I've started examining, one at a time, those various morals and perceptions and habits that I have collected over the past twenty-two years. I look these things over very carefully, and I try to choose the ones that should retain an integral position in my psyche. And likewise I try to discard those that seem to gather like cultural dust piling up on unsuspecting shoulders. I also look around me at the other alternatives available to me, seeking out those things that might possibly fill my gaps.

Slowly has evolved this picture of myself that contains a somewhat compact unity. There exists a definite pattern that I can work from—that I can say is me. And I think this is a very important tool for a human being to develop. The discovery of self, I guess you'd say. So after sorting through the million and one options available, I am able to definitely identify the world that I choose to participate in:

It is a world of simplicity. In a very deliberate way it is naive. It is guided by an attitude of wonder, of discriminatory sensitivity, of the experience and expression of beauty—both in joy and in pain. It concerns itself mainly with what is good, with what is real in myself, in my world, but most importantly in the people I share with. In this idealistic realm, I cannot totally disregard or ignore the petty, or the unreal, or the evil if you will; but I need do no more than to simply acknowledge it. I want no involvement beyond that.

It took a lot of time, a lot of internal debate, to determine that this attitude is really a valid, acceptable reality from which to work. What is reality anyway but the parts of this overwhelmingly vast universe that we allow to pass through our psychic filters.

I have found that a person who functions with that type of an attitude is often taken advantage of. But more importantly, I see that, when becoming involved in this type of sensitivity, one finds himself sometimes to be a carrier of important information. Or finds within himself certain capabilities of insight which really can be beneficial in so many social situations, though such commitments will most certainly cause stress and unnecessary discomforts.

So now I guess I have to decide to what degree I can function as an individual, as a self-full person. What are my priorities concerning me and not-me?

· · · · · · ·

Dad,

As intensely involved as I am these long, fall days, and as incredibly busy as I know you are building a new house in your woods, a year might have passed as easily as the month since last we shared any time.

School is really going well. I managed to select a group of classes and teachers that all share a very specified correlation with me and with each other, so my studies are all focused in one direction, without being spread out all over the academic world of thought. That way when I study I don't have the distraction of trying to shift my state of mind from, say, an art sensitivity course to an all-too-concrete chemistry exam.

All my classes involve a very intense need to just sit and let my ideas and feelings be organized deep within. So my discipline is simply in trusting myself enough, and being open and patient enough, to let these things develop and make themselves known. And then to put them down on paper or however I choose to relate them. Sounds easy, doesn't it? Sure.

I am taking a myth, dreams and creativity class (Fromm, Jung, Campbell), an art forms and ideas class (from one of the finest men I've ever met), a music appreciation course (learning how to listen, not play), and a course entitled Spaceship Earth. Also I'm doing an independent study in humanities, and this is where you come in.

It has become very important to me to try to come to some understanding as to why people are drawn or driven to create, to express, to imagine, to sensualize innerness. Is it beauty or pain or emotion, or a search for meaning? Is it communication or God or is it all these things? So I'm talking to a lot of artists, musicians, dancers, architects, writers. And I'm looking at a lot of artwork, listening to music, being quiet.

If you've the time and the desire, sit down and tell me what is going on between your piano and you. How it feels to play. How it feels not to play. To listen. To play for others, with others. And maybe other arts too. How it feels to build a house or a bookshelf. How you are affected by a photograph or a book or a painting, a song. The approach is endless. I would really value anything you can offer.

If you're in town, you must come by work or the house. Whenever the time is right. I think of you often.

Paul

Dear Paul,

Your news about school is very exciting; I congratulate you. I'm fascinated with your searchings relative to creativity and expression. It's an area in my contemplative life that I find elusive, and I feel somewhat weak in trying to put any of my thoughts into meaningful words—but I'll give it a try.

My perception of the very personal experience of making music at the piano is a glorious one: one of the most singularly rewarding things in my life. It feels good when no other ears but mine are hearing it; it feels good (in a slightly different way) when I play for others. As you know, I see myself as a competent and sensitive player when I take the notes off a printed page; I'm probably a better-than-average sight-reader, resulting from all those years playing church organ.

What I most dearly hope for now is growth into a place where I can do my own versions, original treatments of old standard tunes, extemporaneously. By ear, as we say. I must have several thousand of these preserved in my memory, plus a set of "comfortable" or "right" treatments and harmonies for each of them. And I have adequate skill in my fingers to execute these wonderful sounds. What I don't yet possess—and desperately hope is in there somewhere, dormantly—is the ability to couple these silent but sensed sounds to the tips of my fingers, so I can hear them—audibly.

Thinking back, I see myself as largely self-taught on the piano—in spite of the hundreds and hundreds of lessons I had. The really important stuff I figured out for myself. Like Chopin. (I'm not comparing my talent to his!) Although he had the best teachers of his time, he quickly overtook them, and had to forge ahead, alone, into new and nebulous, uncharted terrain. I suspect that the teachers I was exposed to in Norton, Kansas during the thirties were not comparable to Chopin's, either!

Which brings me to another truism which seems more and more valid to me as the years pass: I find that nearly all really important skills

45

can be learned—but not taught. I've experienced this over and over in dozens of fields. How do you feel about that?

Another observation, while we're on the subject. As I contemplate our "accomplishments", yours and mine, I suspect that we are blessed/cursed with the same internal urging: the one that says "I'm not interested in knowing the accepted, the right way of doing something; I want to invent my own way." This comes upon me if I'm playing the piano, building a simple piece of furniture, chopping wood, or almost any activity you can think of.

Well, as a result, we both have found ourselves reinventing the wheel (but in inferior ways) many times—wasting time and energy by consciously blinding ourselves to the efforts and findings of so many others before us. Is this unwise of us? Perhaps. But, then comes that magic time when we really do create something unique, and worthy. I think it makes all the struggle worthwhile, after all. I'd be interested in knowing how you react to some of this.

Our lives here are very full these days—trying to get this house ready for winter. Let's stay in touch.

> Hurriedly,
> Dad

In class today, there was discussion about narcissism, about the emphasis now being put on the individual — and the importance of coming to terms with oneself. I hesitate to try to come to any conclusions about this because I am obviously at such an extreme ebb when it comes to dealing with people. I think one day I will find that my power lies in my ability to be with myself. What more basic foundation can one work from? But I am also beginning, almost in a sort of panic, to see the incredible importance of incorporating that knowledge into the whole. It is one of those fine lines I have so often heard discussed: to truly have oneself, but also to be able to share oneself unconditionally with those other entities we find surrounding us. The need for this becomes obvious when one realizes he could hardly survive for a week without the knowledge and support of other humans—past and present.

It must be painfully apparent that one of my major goals is to have this capability to share, without hesitation or doubt. I cannot understand why the task is so overwhelmingly difficult. All I know is that the few times I have truly touched and been touched by another person—those few times when I have really seen, and likewise been acknowledged as a reality and not a projection—the reward, the pure exhilarating freshness, was unmistakable.

. . . .

Today is a cold silent day. The air is thin, the sun is weak and dull. I sense some type of primal fear in people. Perhaps we sense a coming storm.

People are drawing together. No one wants to be alone, and today we seem to be dealing on a very base level, far beyond the reach of the mind; it is cell deep. It is a very good thing to see. There is a power moving us today that overrides anything petty, neurotic, or selfish. We are affected as a race.

In a relationship with any degree of intensity, after being with a person for a while, after caring for a person for a while, I begin to read fairly deeply into their being. I begin to formulate or reinforce ideas and preconceptions about who they are, how they function as human beings, what is wrong or right about their attitudes and behavior— *how they ought to change.* I begin anticipating actions and reactions. I start acting toward that person, very deliberately and with all good intention, in such a way as I feel will be beneficial in modifying their behavior.

What most people fail to understand, is that usually we want to see the other person's life changed in a way that suits *our* ideals and requirements, rather than the needs of the person being changed.

Somehow it seems to me that there really is no reason to be so consciously deliberate, so contrived, in the ways in which we try to improve ourselves. The world today is far too psychologically oriented. All our actions, thoughts, relationships seem to need to be carefully observed, analyzed and manipulated toward some preconceived end.

I don't like to be approached in that way, as some type of scholarly exercise in human psychology, and I don't want to run my life that way. I think there is an easier, more graceful way.

I've always felt very strongly against following any prescribed techniques or philosophies for "finding oneself." If there's got to be a book of rules, I want to figure it out for myself. But that way seems to leave a lot of empty spaces where I don't know where to go for an answer, don't know how to act, and I spend a lot of time waiting, watching and wondering—trying to keep a spark alive until the fire is somehow rekindled. Having nothing but a blind trust in myself to carry me through emptiness.

. . . .

It is true, so true, that we choose to be lonely; we make the world of alone.

Thinking back on my past, I find many reasons why this has been so for me. Part of it comes from my experiences of being physically alone. I spent my summers, and some of my falls, for five or six years, working for a guide in northern Colorado. We would be far into the wilderness sometimes for two or three months in a row, without seeing a car or radio or toilet, or the straight lines of a building. It was not unusual for me to spend five or six days at a time, wandering alone, without seeing another soul.

In many ways the experience of being out in the wild is a much more valid lesson in humanity than being in a city. A large city like New York is one hundred percent human-ness; there is nothing else; you are overcome by the totality. In the woods, there is nothing human but you. If something is wrong, out of balance, it can only be you, and your thoughts. The purest of human confrontation!

Probably the strongest source I have for these feelings is Dad. He is dogmatically a loner.

He was a goal-oriented, wordy, intellectual, progressive, successful executive (with a few subtle deviations) until the age of forty-seven. He then abruptly quit his job, sold everything he owned, cut off all of his relationships, including his parents, bought a piece of secluded land in southwest Colorado, and built, almost single-handedly,

```
          CHICKERING BOOKSTORE, INC
             203 SOUTH 2ND STREET
              LARAMIE, WY 82070
               (307) 742-8609

           03:09 pm  Wed 28 May 1997
               Register No. 1

          * - Non Taxable Items

RESTLESS MIND, QUIET THOUGHTS
    1883991072      1 @   12.95    12.95
    Total Items:    1

                 Sub-Total :       12.95
                       Tax :        0.78
                     Total :       13.73
CASH                 13.73
              Total Tendered :     13.73

THANK YOU FOR SHOPPING AT CHICKERING!
```

CHICKERING BOOKSTORE, INC.
203 SOUTH 2ND STREET
LARAMIE, WY 82070
(307) 742-8609

03:09 pm Wed 28 May 1997
Register No. 1

* - Non Taxable Items

RESTLESS MIND, QUIET THOUGHTS
1883991072   1 @ 12.95   12.95
         Total Items: 1

Sub-Total   :   12.95
Tax   :   0.78
Total   :   13.73
CASH   13.73
Total Tendered :   13.73

THANK YOU FOR SHOPPING AT CHICKERING!

a very beautiful home. He spends much of his time reading, playing his piano, organ or harpsichord, snow-shoeing, building furniture—and most of all just sitting. His wife is his sole companion. He is snowed in for weeks each winter. When he does come to town, it is only out of necessity.

He obviously *chose* this lifestyle. He is perfectly capable of being with people; he built his business around it; but he has become so sensitive that he can hardly tolerate his own pain or beauty, much less anyone else's. At times he can be very hard to be with; one has no choice but honesty. He has also dropped the role of father. Instead I have found a place as one of his few friends, which was a very strange transition for me to make.

The point is that, through his choice for aloneness—his unadulterated selfishness, he has found his place in life: his balance, his contentment, his reality.

Loneliness does not have to be synonymous with fear.

· · · · · · ·

Well, I still live here in Durango—spending my time working as a waiter in two restaurants. Never expected to find myself in exactly this situation—the challenge of a gourmet, tuxedo, tray-service, table-side-cooking type of situation which requires the utmost concentration and assertiveness on my part. But money is very scarce now, and so, at least for right now, I think I should focus my time on paying some bills and saving for my next big change.

The rest of my time, it seems, is being spent exploring the strange and vast, alluring and frightening realms of another person, Cindy—and the connection there is to be had, or made.

As usual, love is so strong, so important, so much more frightening and exciting for me than it seems to be for anyone else. At times I feel foolish because I am so affected, so stifled and so inspired; I am such a hopeless romantic. But I've always felt that intensity of any kind was an affirmative gesture. So I can feel assured when I more or less give my life, at the present, to another person, and center my learning abilities at exploring just what it all entails: the differences, the compromises, the surprises and disappointments. The pain and the pleasure.

So much of it frightens me. I can sometimes see how enveloped I and she are by our petty importances, by the joy to be found, and the potency, when two people connect at that level.

Not having a home now causes some concerns. Because my possessions, my toys, my reminders of myself, are all packed away, so that all of the things that I do normally to be Paul—writing, my woodwork, my plants, my house—are nonexistent; sometimes I feel almost nonexistent myself. Perhaps it's better though, for now I live with Cindy in her home, and I can fully focus myself on her and what this all means. A worthy sacrifice.

Leslie is still here, but will be leaving for Denver and more schooling in a month. She has been so fine to me lately. So strong and supportive with my silly disorientation and doubt.

. . . .

Cindy.

Where to begin? Knowing that she and my involvement with her are the most important, exciting, captivating part of my being right now, and feeling somehow the need to come to terms with this wonder-full thing that is happening to me.

So it's all come about so quickly and easily; it's surprisingly powerful and oh-so-sweet. Perhaps I've never felt such affirmative feelings for anyone, anything. I think that it's really love, beyond me, beyond her. Some exquisite connection of compassion and understanding and inspiration.

Sometimes I feel I'm so infatuated because it's just in my nature to be so. But when I'm not afraid, and when I'm with her, I know it's real, and just *that knowing* is all the proof I need. Though my head really spins, my knees grow weak, my heart pounds, my face flushes; it's like living in a fairy tale, a water-color world—and I would like to examine it, to explore my own impressions, my hopes, fears, expectations. I want to tap this incredible exhilaration, because—well, because it's so fine, so strong, so out-of-the-blue.

Who is this girl?

She seems to somehow come closer than anyone I've ever met to living and understanding a reality like mine. Almost everything positive or affirmative sought after by me seems to be encompassed in her. Perhaps that's why I gain so much strength being with her. Adventure, romanticism, casualness, intensity, naiveté, independence, playfulness, wonder, calmness; the list goes on and on. So far, so little that I see seems weak or negative. Anything I find wrong seems so unimportant, and most likely is me. How can that be? I know myself well enough to know that I am easily infatuated. People become my gods. But lovers are different. I always keep my guard up, taking care, watching, holding back, expecting nothing, usually in doubt.

Now I am in awe. Animated, excited, inspired. Almost never have I trusted so much. Nothing is happening in my life but Cindy, and I (the total skeptic) am absolutely captivated. I'm thankful every day, if only for fresh memories, fresh dreams. So fine! My love is so fine.

To lie by her side in the night or the morning, dark against the sheets, and warm. Watching the sleepy motions and rhythms of her body, wanting always to reach out and run my hands over her skin, knowing the magic of touch—mine and hers.

So peaceful and rich, just to watch as she lies asleep. Looking at her sweet sweet face, so alive, relaxed, alluring. Thrilling as she shifts and moves in tight against my side; I just can't get close enough, she says. Becoming light-headed now with my love, feeling her feeling me, pounding heart in passions awakening, becoming enveloped in the timelessness and mystery of our love-making, my lust makes my head spin, my ears ring, my body tingle and buzz.

Enchanted by her sleepy reverie, her soft words, soft glances, gentle caresses, laughter and sighs. Our time goes on like clouds across the open sky.

Feeling now the responsibility of her trust, holding her heart in my hands like a dewdrop, fragile and clear. Hoping she realizes that she has mine also, raw and tender; hoping, too, that she sees it as a gift and not a burden.

· · · · · · ·

Most of my time lately has been with Cindy. It became easy to forget myself and give in to another reality. But not so easy to assume responsibility for the effects of such a decision.

With time and patience and an acknowledgment of the depth of my ignorance, though, the confusion is paying off, and I find myself on a new level of understanding through my involvement with another human being. Food for faith, and new incentive for a truly compassionate attitude.

· · · · · · ·

Mid-afternoon at Turtle Lake now, sitting on a rock in water that sweeps by me in lines of light and dark, the sky an offset reflection. Ducks skim the surface, snakes and turtles and other strange things swim up out of the depths and peer out at me as if I, some grotesque aberration from another time and place, have no right to exist in their world.

I've thought lots about the conundrum of relating to another person. Not to possess or define, nor to explain or describe that person. But to understand: maybe like, hopefully love, and, I would add, respect. But that's a pretty easy one. That's just an Introduction To Compassion 101.

People have certainly been on my mind now. A couple of years ago, I seemed to have forgotten myself, and switched my emphasis and regard to those around me. I've become ridiculously extravagant with the energy I have to give off to the world, and pretty tight with sharing any with myself. But I'm beginning to see tendencies of healthy greed welling up.

Now I find myself involved totally in this one-on-one situation, and it seems to be contrary to what I would have thought. Thus I can take all the energy I have available for sharing with others, and direct it like a laser into this one soft and gentle, child-like lady who has, by one of those all too frequent but still freak accidents of nature, chosen to do the same thing with me.

It really touches me to think that I might feel some joy with another person; it's not them that gives me joy, it's my own feeling.

So true, but so lonely. Sometimes I lie in bed with Cindy, and watch her sleep, or waken, and I almost think that I'm her.

Well, shit, why not. We can travel through space, soon we shall travel to other times, why can't I be able to experience other people?

· · · · · · ·

Squatting here by Junction Creek, skin to stone and sun, ears to water (there's not much, but what's here can certainly carry a tune), eyes to empty page, and mind way out in space. It's good for me to write sometimes when I really don't want to. When I feel stupid or silly or crazy. Or nothing at all. I certainly have to try then to squeeze something meaningful from my presence—my present presence.

Saw a fresh young colt today, standing steaming in cold air and dry grass. Made me think of a dream of a dream that I had: A young guy, four or five, maybe more. This young one, silent and stare-eyed, blank faced, living in a brown adobe brick room, dirt floors the same color as the walls, dusty air the same color as the floor, as his face, his hands, his hair, his mother, his life. It's dry and brown outside too. No wind, no color, just a brown sun in a brown sky on brown earth. Hard, dry and brown. Everything. Everybody. Everywhere.

He lays his dusty body down naked, on the floor, and dreams: of the ocean, blue even in the moonlight, the foam on the crest of the waves and the foam blowing and rolling in balls up the beach, silver and alive. The sky clear and blue, even in the moonlight. Then, a horse: silver, its mane blowing silver and alive. Himself, snow white, iridescently glowing, eyes of blue and hair of silver. Flying high on a horse over waves in the wind, singing. It begins to rain light and water. He wakes, crying and choking.

And I awaken, hard and dry—the dream forgotten until I see this small colt, suckling and soft and so sure.

· · · · · · ·

Late at night, dark and quiet, except for the streetlight shining through the cracks in our door, and the gurglings of the fish tank. Unable to sleep. So strange for me. So often, most often, my bed is my salvation. Like a drunk with his bottle, at times before noon I am longing for my bed asleep, alone, safely naive and unresponsible.

But not tonight. No, there are too many questions, angry questions, fearful questions, restless taunting doubts that will ultimately lead to sadness, unresolved and undefined. Too potent to ignore. Too painful to acknowledge, like some chronic human itch.

I slip out of our bed, not wanting to waken Cindy, not wanting her to worry, to cheat her of the soothing sleep and happy dreams she has.

Yet needing her to care. Needing her touch, a reminder I am real, and not just some misbegotten idea in someone's warped mind. But no, she sleeps on, so soft and so sweet. I melt for a moment, tempted to take her in my arms and whisper something silly. But no, my brain throbs on.

I light a candle, which throws quiet light around the room, illuminating those objects around me which somehow are me, so elusive and intangible. A twinge of mortality runs through me, deep. I think perhaps to call someone, to demand solace and reassurance that everything is fine.

But luckily it's too late. Else I might—I probably would—just be shown the frustration of non-understanding, the distance between minds. And of course, I would find that everything is not fine.

So glad to have my journal; it works somehow as dialogue, not monologue, and I am relieved.

Paul had discussed with me his concern over Cindy's unplanned conception at this time. Then his journal revealed a very brief, eloquent reflection on this magical happening.

Beguiled, entranced by the pristine emotions remembered in a warm, dark bed: the subtle, cellular connection of skin on skin, a sweet soft kiss that penetrates down into the caverns of the unconsciousness, tapping a volcano of headspinning passion which erupts with the power of a hundred thousand generations of men, striving for immortality.

A tiny flicker of life, an inaudible hum of heartbeat and breath begins, a whisper of form and idea and emotion is heard, deep inside a woman, young and scared—swept away by the sudden wave of truth which floods through her life, tearing reality from its mooring, and sweeping it off, leaving her standing, stranded on a ghostly shore of harsh, entropic insight.

A trying situation for these young lovers to face. I know they agonized over how best to respond, together. Finally, they decided on an abortion. Paul maintained his part of the partnership with compassion and gentleness, travelling with Cindy to the selected place in Albuquerque. They managed to keep their respect for each other intact.

I Choose Beauty

The Twenty-fourth Year

I *could sense that Paul felt the pressure for decisive change building, on several fronts. His education, his career plans, his lover, his total path all seemed at a crossroads, and he struggled to find the right direction.*

I don't really have anything to say, but it's been a while and I know I have to make a special effort to somehow shine through this drabness of spirit that seems to pervade humanity these days. It's evident everywhere: the majority of people I know are all sick, painfully horribly sick, classes are empty, faces are empty, the streets are quiet; even the little things we do to burden ourselves and create some form of disorder are meaningless. I know, too, at times like this, that lots of time is spent in bed. Dreamers are sleeping, lovers are holding on tight to each other, and lonely ones to themselves.

. . . .

Some of my best times in the Fall have been the months of those years I spent far in the woods, mostly alone and not concerned by much except not stubbing my toes or getting knocked down by a falling tree, or struck by lightning or mauled by a rabid rabbit.

I remember one of those times—as clear as yesterday. It is November; I'm camped deep in the Mount Zirkel Wilderness. It is three o'clock in the morning. I awaken into thought like diving into a clear, icy pool. I pull my well-worn clothes from the pocket of warmth at the bottom of my sleeping bag, rise, and dress quickly.

Unzipping the tent I step out into the night. A crystalline world silenced by the cold, overwhelmed by the brilliance of a hundred million stars. Forcing my fingers into animation, I light a fire, the flame fighting passionately against the cold. I pile on some logs, start coffee, light a lantern, and set out with a bucket across the meadow at whose border we have camped.

The snow is already knee-deep. The sound of my boots breaking through the frozen crust echoes off the trees, echoes off the mountains towering above, and is absorbed into the endless, empty air.

The horses are huddled together. I can feel their cooperative warmth from yards away. I feel guilty awakening them, but drowsy, they allow themselves to be led, one by one, down to the stream to drink. I fill my bucket, and spread out some hay for them.

Back at camp I split wood and start fires for breakfast. Frozen eggs won't fry in frozen oil, so it's boiled eggs, venison, hot cakes, hot fruit, coffee. The air fills with smells and the men wake up, boisterous, anticipating. We eat quickly, not wanting to stop moving for long. I clean up, pack lunches, close up the tents, and we set out through the forest, winding up our boot-beaten trail which leads up the mountainside. We move slowly. Stiffened bodies move awkwardly through darkness and cold, and maybe a little fear.

We go a-hunting. I alone carry no gun. I have killed once, and have never known greater shame. The time passes and we continue to trudge up the slope. As bodies loosen and warm, so also the spirit of excitement picks up. I leave the men off at various spots along the way. Here they will sit and smoke, weave hero fantasies, wait. It will be my job to keep moving. To beat the woods, to create fear so the elk will run, forgetting to look ahead.

But I am no hunter. It is all just a sad joke to me. I am really a spy for the other side. As soon as I leave the last man behind, I circle around and head back to camp for a few hours more sleep, a book, some quiet thought.

The sky is becoming light. I stop on a rock overlooking a large meadow, to watch the sun rise. Shadows are thrown across the forest below, across trees, across streams, across mountains. I look out over the vast expanse of textured wilderness that has been my home for the past five months. And it looks back at me.

A rifle shot crashes through my thoughts. And another and another. I look below me and see the bright orange clothing of a group of hunters moving through the trees. Two large bull elk gallop out into the middle of the meadow. They stop, sides heaving, foaming, wild-eyed, paralyzed by fear and confusion. This is not part of their reality. The hunters move closer, not seeing the elk through the trees. From the other side of the meadow another orange vest approaches, unaware but wary. Closer and closer they converge on the meadow, and the elk still stand in fright.

I jump up and down on my perch, waving and shouting. Run goddammit run. The hunters are almost to the edge of the trees. I run down the slope and into the meadow, heading straight for the elk, yelling and shouting. They take heed and run into the trees, followed by a terrible volley of gunfire as the hunters come out into the open. But they are too late. And I, exultant, make my own quick escape, laughing hysterically, followed by a volley of outraged abuse and verbal bullets. I'd never make it in a war, I guess.

· · · · · · ·

Nowadays I just spend time with my silly little artifacts. Cindy's birthday is coming up, and I can hardly wait till she's asleep, so I can creep out of bed and quietly sand on wood, or draw little shapes or cut out the bits and pieces I will need to create, to put together, somehow, this most powerful form of expression of love and humanness that, in spite of its clumsiness and inconsequence, is still the most eloquent thing I can do.

· · · · · · ·

Riding home, a truck passes me by. Two large greasy men in a truck, making obscene remarks, sneering and hating and crying out for release. I reply in kind. They stop the truck and give chase on foot, futilely.

I ride off, laughing, sort of. I go home, change clothes and ride down to the store. My mind is elsewhere as I walk out the door. Then, a fist in my face. Shouting and swearing and punching at me. Two ugly, violent deadly men.

Horrible fear, hatred, and finally sadness. Resignation I feel at the hopelessness of communicating, of understanding at all. Finally I come home, cry a bit, and the world suddenly begins anew as I put the finishing touches to Cindy's birthday gift. Triumph, exhilarating triumph makes my head buzz. I become agitated and excited by my success.

I go for a run in the country to calm myself. Glad to have legs and lungs and energy; feeling refreshed I dance along.

But a car screams by, close and fast, hurtling abuses as it passes. All my previous anger and frustration wells up. I have visions of violence, of blood, of terrible brutal satisfaction. Then my pace slows, my legs ache, my lungs reach for air. I feel old, silly, useless.

Home again, a hot bath, dinner and wine, I begin to revive. It's so easy to forget. Now I'm really ready to study; damn, but this stuff is fascinating, eh, and really meaningful too. And my mind is surging forward like twenty horses. But the house is quiet. The air gets cold, I am alone, lonely. Shit, I never used to get lonely. Am I getting old, weak, spiritless? When I get lonely, everything I do seems to be distraction. I hate it. I get restless, anxious, angry.

So many feelings! All so strong, so sick, so overwhelming, so distant, too. I feel like I've been through a dough machine. But now I can sleep. Hide for a while, let the world move beneath me, around me, as it wills.

And tomorrow?

. . . .

Riding up Wildcat Canyon road today with a special friend, we talked of those people in our lives who were extra important, influential, helpful. People who in many cases were more family than family. That there really is a larger family that we all are a part of, and those folks involved were easily distinguished from the multitude of friends and lovers and acquaintances we have.

Then the wind came roaring down the road as we broke out of the canyon and into the open, a fierce bitter wind that made conversation, and almost consciousness, impossible. I retreated far away from sensations, deep into my thoughts. I thought of those folks in my life that seemed to serve as teachers, as inspired examples, almost as human deity, far beyond the impact of most other people involved as my family.

Three people stand out in my mind as being very important. Why are they, what is it they possess, what are those qualities I admire so much? Is it even right to hold individuals in such high regard? Is it fair to them? Fortunately for my self-respect, these are people who have also provoked the admiration and awe of others, so I am not alone in my feelings.

One is my father, who suffered the life of mundane urban mediocrity and the emptiness of the business world, the automation of his society, until the age of forty-seven, when he gladly dumped it all for a solitary life of quiet introspection and creative expression. He is a man of the highest caliber, and, by far, my best friend. It's so fine to feel so, for my father; I realize how rare it really is.

The second is my favorite professor, Weston: he seems to create his art so smoothly and naturally; of course, I have so little understanding of it at all. It's nice to know, though, that these connections can happen totally regardless of my shallow, clumsy attempts at forming my life.

The third is Andy—slightly younger than I—a musician. To an extreme degree, he involves himself with music just as the professor involves himself with painting. My father is both musician and craftsman, and rationalé exquisité.

I think perhaps the major thing that draws me to these people, is their intense and so rare awareness of the illusion of our lives; yet they maintain, they thrive on, and even generate an incredible responsiveness and excitement to that very illusion. They use it as their tool, their power.

They are finely tuned, both to themselves and to that which exists around, in conjunction with, and in spite of, themselves.

These three are so calm, yet so energetic. They seem so close to themselves, and seem to dearly value the time they spend alone. Still, compassion is their guiding light. Tolerance and understanding, and an exquisite ability to listen and learn from others, makes them favorites among the people who know them.

They are constantly challenged and can throw themselves into the drabbest of situations with a vitality and curiosity that truly amazes me. They are easy and free of time. Spontaneous, yet meticulous. They seem so free.

· · · · · · ·

There is a state of mind I sometimes find myself in, a state very much like the abandon found in bicycling, the same space involved in creative activity, in which I relinquish the incompetence of my deliberate efforts at organizing or rationally directing myself. I don't give up thinking; I just let my thoughts, my actions, and my answers come of themselves. I have to trust my inner abilities to understand and I have to feel good about waiting.

Tonight I think I feel a story forming within me; if I'm lucky, after acknowledging the first few sentences, the rest will simply appear. I think I'll try to get it down on paper:

It was a grey summer morning. A warm rain drizzled down, dripping off swollen trees. A few birds chirped, but otherwise there was no sound. No wind danced across the landscape.

A jeep came rambling up the road, bouncing and swerving, and slammed on its brakes when it came to the fork in the road. A young man hopped out: slim, blond, in his mid-twenties. He waved his hand and the jeep screeched off up the road, leaving him in a cloud of misty quiet.

He looked back down the road for a long time, then shouldered his small pack and headed up the smaller of two roads. He walked at a steady pace for a few hours, until the road turned into two ruts, and then into a small path that wound its way into the thick of the trees, climbing up through the forest.

He slowed down a bit, but kept on walking, soaked through by the wet underbrush and the warm misty drizzle that floated down through the trees. Head down, hands in pockets, he looked about him, little absorbed in watching the ground before his feet, listening to the noises inside his head.

61

At one point he caught the sound of hoofbeats coming down the trail in front of him. He turned off and hid in the brush as a small group of riders and pack horses paraded by him and down toward the road. When they had passed, he continued on his way, a little faster and a little more attentive, higher and farther into the mountains.

By mid-afternoon the rain had stopped, the sky cleared, the sun streaked down, bathing the forest floor in a mosaic of shadow and light. He came to a river, steaming in the sun. A clear, musical stream, flowing from deep pool to deep pool, covered with sticks and leaves and the bottom of the sky.

There the man stopped for the first time. He pulled off his clothes, plunged in and out of the water quickly, drank a bit, and then lay in the sun to dry. Refreshed and relaxed, he stretched out on a rock, gazing up into the sky at the clouds floating by, listening to the water, feeling the turning of the earth beneath him. He lay like this for a long time, passively, letting the motion and the rhythm of change clear his muddy thoughts, and for a while he forgot himself.

Soon, though, little hobgoblins of thought came creeping out from the corners of his mind, poking and pinching at his brain. Growing restless he rose and dressed, and set off once again, following the river now, leaving the trail behind in the past.

By nighttime he was miles into the wilderness. He came to a spot where the river suddenly dropped off the rocks a hundred feet or so above him, plunging into a luminous pool nestled in a bed of granite at his feet. He climbed to the top and stretched out beneath a tree at the water's edge, lost in its power and its roar. The moon came out with a chill. He carried no sleeping bag, but built a small fire and wrapped himself around it.

All night long he squatted by this tiny fire, feeding it sticks, listening to the water, the breeze in the trees, the moonlight, birds and creatures of night which came to the edge of the brush and watched him with glowing eyes from the shadows. His brain roared with a fury greater than that of the river.

Morning found him still awake, but dazed, staring into the bed of coals. He went to the edge of the water and bent over a pool to splash some on his face. His reflection was a cruel shock, and he jerked back, afraid of that vacant image that he found. He ran out into the trees, intensely agitated. He walked around and around, pacing, swallowing hard to suppress the intensity of emotion he felt would overwhelm him.

Finally the sun and the trees and the motion calmed him somewhat. He spent the rest of the day walking through the forest, watching as closely as he could the trees and rocks and grasses. He looked intensely at the shadows that they cast. They seemed to mean something important.

When the darkness rolled in again, he was full and satisfied, his mind had somewhat cleared and he felt he could sit and finally sort through his thoughts. He gathered some wood and built himself a small fire again. Sitting in its glow he began to talk and sing: to himself, to the trees, to the stars— sometimes with words and sometimes just with sweet noises that felt good to be shared. He was trying to explain himself in any way he could.

He did this until he was hoarse, and then, feeling the total culmination of a lifetime's emotion rolling over him, he leaned up against a tree at the edge of the firelight and cried longer and harder and deeper than he had ever known possible. He cried until the world dissolved around him, until he was gone— evaporated, and all that existed was a feeling. Finally, exhausted and spent, he lay down by his fire and slept.

The sun was high and warm when he woke. He rose, clear-eyed, easy, empty of mind. He went to the river to cleanse his face. This time he gazed long into the water, deep into his eyes. Looking into his eyes looking into infinity.

Then he went to the edge of the rocks, and with a long graceful leap, jumped out off the cliff and shattered on the granite below at the edge of the stream.

. . . .

Once again, I seek out the heights. How strange, for years I was unable to be in high places. Climbing up mountains, looking out and up—it always made me cry. Now it seems to be where I always end up—perhaps I'm seeking the tears. But more, I think, I seek some time of totality. The wind is always blowing hard. I blow with it, diffuse and thoughtless. The sun beats down so surely. Still, there is coldness, the biting shock of *realness*. How strange that, as a human, in my world exists *un*realness?

Walking through the brush, though, is very real. Any unreality is mine, and it becomes so evident. So I watch and listen, and step softly. It feels good when an animal is spooked. I am acknowledged; I must be real.

The little shoots and buds remind me of how glad I am it is spring. The bird-song and the clouds. How glad, too, must be the elk and the deer. How sweet those first fresh bites of greenness.

How much easier it might be if my failure was one of survival. An animal lives; if he can't, he dies. A human, though, has so many more dimensions to his existence. So many choices. Animals belong to the world of beauty. Even in death, except, perhaps, for road kill: man again. Still, I too choose beauty. I can acknowledge ugliness, but I cannot seek it, or use it as a tool. I can be frightened by it, but I shall not be overcome.

· · · · · · ·

I ride along the valley edge, keeping my eyes to the ridgeside. So many animals: deer, elk, birds, varmints, so close to man, even counting on him now, for survival.

Most people dislike this. Some are irritated, some afraid; some see it is a sign of the decline of the earth, a sign of weakness. Perhaps it is, in a way. The end of wildness. But what is wild, at least in part, but a fear: fear of each other, the unknown in each other. We needn't be wild to be free. I myself, in comparison with the majority of other humans, I would consider to be wild. Yet I live as all others do, with them, by them, for them. I have found that there is more, though. More than man and his things. Much more.

Perhaps this seeming docileness in the animals, especially the deer and elk, is actually a sign of friendliness, a trend towards cohabitation. Realizing, somehow, that we must share in order to survive; perhaps what we see is the beginning of a natural process of transition toward an "Eden" kind of trust and integration. I would love to see deer in the parks, elk on the golf course, grazing.

If they can only learn of man, especially his uncontrolled power. If they can only be patient with our deceptions, illusions and misunderstanding. And if we can only learn to love them, to acknowledge their importance and validity, their reality.

. . . .

Dad,

Hi! I don't know if I liked this card cause I wanted to write you, or if I felt like writing cause I liked the card, but it is a pretty one, yes? How do your days pass you by? Maybe thickly and oppressively—or lightly and full of wonder? Are you weary or is there importance to what you do?

I am moving along at supersonic speed, sailing through confusion and fear like some squawking bird flapping frantically through the clouds, grey wet silent clouds. I rise every morning and fumble my way through this haze to work, where I struggle hard and sweat much as the minutes pass by, unendingly by. And then home to whatever habit most comfortably bores me to sleep.

But some days the air is clear and I see the elk on the hillsides, and they see me. Someone writes me a letter, or looks me into my eyes, or yells at me or something—lights at the end of the tunnel and all that. Mom called and said I could have the money from Gramp's bequest anytime. So as soon as I finish the greenhouse I'm building, I think I'll go to Denver for a few days, perhaps buy a car and take a couple of weeks and see some people and places that might do me good.

It looks like maybe Cindy and I will be parting ways soon, and I'd sure like to have some strength and clarity inside of me before I do battle with such strange, awkward pain. I'd like to come out and spend a couple of days with you.

If you need some work done we could do it then. Or maybe just go for long hikes and see if we can find any hidden buds and blossoms sneaking out early in the sun.

See you soon,
Paul

Paul came out to spend a few days with me; we had several deep and rewarding talks. It seemed to me that, through all of his pain and confusion, he was slowly building stability—and direction. I was optimistic about him, perhaps more so than I had been for a long while.

He was beginning to feel that his time at Fort Lewis College should come to a close; it was not yielding what it should for him any longer. He had been quite impressed with what he saw at the University of California at Santa Cruz, and spoke more and more frequently of transferring there to complete his education. And he did part ways with Cindy; it was a period of transition.

Well, I'm still sitting here quietly in Durango, moving pretty slowly, trying to be calm and come to terms with myself before trying to take on the rest of the world. I guess there are not too many drastic changes to speak of in life. But some of my friends might find me much different: a little more confident, direct, perhaps a little colder and harder. Life and especially love seems to do that to me. Still, I continue on, sometimes very well and sometimes miserably. It's always pretty debatable whether I will pull it off at all, or not, struggling with elusive, star-struck and vastly out-of-reach ideas. Will my strength outlast my imagination? It should be close.

Building greenhouses and hot tubs right now for a living, waiting on some tables. Not doing much writing, but my artwork stays alive, and always expression is foremost in any situation. Hopefully I can move to Santa Cruz to finish my schoolwork this fall.

． ． ． ． ． ． ．

This young buck is getting ready to migrate west. I'm really not so sure why I have decided to make this change, but the motivation is coming from deep inside, the change is very deliberate, and for the first time in a while, the feelings are strong and true. My destiny has once again gained control—always just in the nick of time.

For once my predominant feeling is excitement, and fear has taken a back seat for the time being (what a relief that is). I look forward to solitude and anonymity. It's been a long, long while since

I've been alone, and I crave it like a fiend. Things are really falling into place, and I trust it.

When Paul told me he had decided to leave Durango and move to Santa Cruz, my heart sank. I guess I knew it had to happen sometime, but I also knew that I would miss having him close by. He left at the end of summer, the summer that marked the deepest connection between us that we had known. He came to visit me just before departing. We said our goodbyes. I watched him drive away over the last ridge, then went inside to my desk and wrote:

A Lasting Image:
The two men stand alone on the hilltop, embracing—not hearing the breeze that stirs the tall trees around them nor seeing the late summer sky overhead. All sensations focus intently at one point. For they are at the moment of parting. It is not the first time, but it is the most painful.

There is an evident kinship between them, though one is much younger, and blond—while the other is greying at hair and beard. Both are lean and tan, and plainly clothed. Long minutes pass, while they stand together; no words are heard—only the sobbing. The feelings deepen, and each writhes inside, trying to wrest free of his shroud of pain—at least a little—but it clings insistently. This pain will not be thrust aside by any effort—nor should it; it is there to be felt, and to be accepted.

But why the special intensity of this moment on the hilltop, against all those countless others, beside countless roads?

Because inside each of them there has now grown a sharply heightened awareness of the other's worth, and of the relationship which has evolved between them. This is a moment which brands a unique and permanent niche into each memory—into each mind and body—a spot that will never be deserted nor relinquished to some new sensation. Branded there by pain—and love.

. . . .

And so, after twenty-four bungled years of opportunity to know and be close to my son, I finally came to the point—after many many painful and confusing experiences/connections/disruptions between us—I came to the position of truly and fully being able to perceive him and appreciate him for the gifted man that he was. Were they wasted years, those first twenty-four of my relative blindness and ignorance? How to say? I guess I don't know how to progress any faster than I know how to. Without all the earlier pain and awkwardness, perhaps I (and we) would never have arrived at the level of love and admiration that we ultimately found. At any rate, I did finally realize what a blessing I possessed—and I never again forgot it.

It's Life and Life Only

The Twenty-fifth Year

For the next several years, we exchanged, mostly in letters, our thoughts and feelings—as never before. Fortunately Paul kept my letters and I kept his. They become more precious to me as the years pass. It was an exchange, I think, that proved not only supremely rewarding, but quite revealing of each of us.

Dear Dad,

My little trailer sits nestled in the moldy California forest, lost in a damp chilled drizzle, encased in a lonely sweeping fog. I wake every morning (thirsty—I have no water; hungry—I have no kitchen; aching—I have no bathroom) and ride through the rain and the redwoods down a steep and narrow, windy, windy and steeper and narrower road, into Santa Cruz, to some small New Age or Born Again or Punk Rocker or Ultra Natural cafe, where I drink and eat and shit (not in that order) and go over my plans for the day.

Satisfied, I hop on my bike, ride through the packed, noisy streets of thousands of glaring staring blaring faces, (riding a bike in this town is no joke; not only is traffic incredible, and the streets very narrow, and every road cut off by bays and rivers and canyons—so that everyway is the long way around; but you should see the women! I'm supposed to keep my eyes and mind on the road?) up through the gates of the university. Instant quiet. Little paths up steep grassy hills into the redwoods, over little redwood bridges above flower-lined streams, looking out across to sea as I break out into the open. Then . . .

Endless lines to stand in, endless forms to fill out, endless housing lists to read, and then back on my bike, across the quiet hills, into the sea of faces, riding around town looking at houses after houses after apartments after condos.

Then some dinner in the same small New Age-Born Again-Punk Rocker-Aux Naturale cafe, and down to the sea. Where I sip on beers and watch the waves crash up on the slime-smocked rocks and the pelicans dive—listen to the sea-lions singing in the waves, like coyotes in the dark.

Then back up the same curvy steep narrow road to my tiny trailer and bed. Different as different can be, and so far so good. Me and the ocean are going to be good friends. I'll write again as soon as I've an address. It shouldn't be long.

Un abrazo (a big hug),
Paul

· · · · · · ·

Dad,

Hello out there. Christ, Colorado seems miles and years and dreams away from here. I'd almost forgotten what it was like (after only two long weeks) until this morning. I woke early, and in my little trailer tucked away beneath the trees and fog, it felt like prehistoric fantasy. I took a long, slow walk along an ancient rusted pair of railroad tracks, that led deep into the misty, dark and mysterious forest, steep hills overgrown with fern and moss, tiny trails winding through shadowy glens of eight-to-ten-foot redwood trunks—tiny brown deer dancing through the threads of sunlight that filter through the trees—raccoons and hawks and butterflies and early morning birdsong, and at the bottom of a deep lonely canyon creeps a deep and lonely river—serene and content.

Now though, I sit here on this Sunday afternoon beach, indented into the fine warm sand, surrounded by dozens and hundreds of people, swimming through the glare of the sunlight off the sand; and out in the bay hundreds of orange and white and yellow and red and blue sailboats, gliding along through the glitter of the sunlight on the sea.

The waves roll in like some ethereal metronome, the gulls screech, and little children shout and shriek as they prance through the foam at the edge of this very great sea.

The challenge of this change and this exceptional aloneness is beginning to work its wonders. I feel so much. Vital sometimes, or destitute and melancholy, or drowning in fear, or soaring in ecstatic exhilaration; profound confusion—sometimes young and sometimes grey and weathered.

Very much me.

I think of you often and, you know, it always brings a smile—not a grin or a smirk, but one big smile.

Paul

Hi,

Got your second letter yesterday; it's a treat to share in some of your new experiences. I'm taking a week off from projects, and just trying to spend a lot of time inside myself—so it feels like a good time to write you.

Fall is here, some bright patches are beginning to show in the oak, and the garden is ready to freeze out. Some of the most beautiful crystally clear days lately that I've ever seen—and a full moon at night. Work is well along on various preparations for winter, and it feels good, getting everything battened down. My shop is somewhat set up in the garage. By the way, I talked to your favorite professor, Weston, on the phone lately; we're to have lunch together Monday. He says the rocking chair you made him is holding together fine, and he loves it.

Most of our vegetables are harvested; we brought in about seventy-five pounds of potatoes, probably an equal amount of tomatoes, also carrots, beans, squash, etc. We've eaten our first chicken—and I think that entire meal was home grown—our first. Even the basil I used in last night's lasagna was ours!

I've thought a lot about you the last few weeks; you've made a huge impression on me—an increasing one. You seem to live your life with

more grace, more dignity (I think that word has a good side), more ease,
than anyone else I know. And I've undoubtedly learned more from you
than from any other person.

I hope that things go well for you there in Santa Cruz, and I wait
eagerly to hear from you.

Lovingly,
Dad

Sitting in a cozy chair by this smoky fire in my new comfortable home, on a chilly, silent, foggy, foggy night—sipping wine, being alone and far from all that I know, looking at some pictures of places and people that are my home; I came across a photo of Irene and me, talking with each other at Leslie's wedding reception. I am looking very out of place in my blue suit coat and white boutonniere, one hand in my pocket and the other gesturing very engagingly between us, emphasizing some vastly important idea as our minds strive to touch one another's. She stands there, straight and serene, beautiful and intent, her eyes penetrating the facade of mine.

I guess that was the last time she and I were together. How long ago it seems. Colorado is so far away. Even here in my house, with the pen scratching and the fire crackling, I can hear the melodious songs of the sea lions through a quarter mile of dense, silent fog. They sound like my friends, the coyotes of the forest.

My life here is very new: the city, the sea, my aloneness (how I used to thrive on that), new beginnings. But I have not changed. Like a sudden movement in a still forest, this switch in reality has made myself very apparent. I am still just Paul.

. . . .

Anxiety sometimes seems to dominate me these days. It clutters my oh-so-short time, befuddles my decisions, weakens my intent, and far overshadows any feeble attempts I make at growth and expression. I certainly won't win any awards for complacency.

School is obviously the center of my life. Not only must it be done with an obsession for integrity and intensity, but all else in my situation must be directed at boosting my academic attempts. Obviously my change of scenery in coming to Santa Cruz is one of my most powerful external tools. I must keep an attitude of freshness, naiveté, perhaps. Involve myself in the new. (Be here new.)

Internally, it is even more difficult. I know the times when I am true, and I must acknowledge those as my signposts. I must wander on with, if not confidence, then at least conviction.

I cannot let loneliness control me, because I know it only compounds the problem, making me fearful, inept, disrespectful. As far as relationships go, I must trust to fate. I know that. Take advantage of this aloneness to better your friendship with *you*. And pay special attention to your present contacts; those are your building blocks.

So I must say to myself: continue to move; your body is your most direct tool, both as translator and as healer; continue to create— ideas, a garden, some woodwork; trust that a job, money, toys, etc. will present themselves when their time arrives. Just be prepared.

And above all, listen to your feelings, and to the feelings around you. Things could become very wonderful.

. . . .

Hello my friend, my journal,

Nothing new, no fabulous insights, no overwhelming revelation, just a tranquil end to a peaceful day. What little anger occurred was gracefully reimbursed by the gentle direct smile of a very lovely lady.

Perhaps I gained a fraction of an inch today, in this vague journey, whose end must surely not even exist yet in the mind of God.

Still, no new questions demanding answers.

I remain.

By this time, Paul knew a lot of my experiences with Primal Therapy; we spoke often about what it meant to me—about the benefits to be had through the allowing of unrestrained expression of feelings. And he was to develop more and more of an appreciation for such tools over the coming years.

Hello Papa,

I've just seen a French movie so my mind is still in Paris. If, when you are in Denver, you find that it is showing, do whatever you can to go see it. It is called "Claire de Femme". The Europeans have a way of penetrating gently to your guts, and both warming them (I guess with the assurance that many people *do* feel) and provoking them (with the reminder that so often that feeling is pain). But they make even pain beautiful.

A line from the film which I found so beautiful that I wrote it on the palm of my hand in the dark so that I would remember: "We live in a time when everyone is screaming loneliness, and no one knows that he is really screaming love". The whole movie is like that.

I thank you for your letter. Aside from this movie, and a couple of other foreign films I've seen—and maybe the sound of the sea-lions barking as I lie in my bed late at night—it is the only piece of realness that I've experienced for quite some time. You know, I get letters from other people, and it just compounds my confusion, my sense of futility, even though their letters are often filled with assurance and proclamations of love.

I guess when I left my home in Durango and left behind all my social habits, and wandered out into this crowded void, I found myself to be overwhelmingly apparent. Which I probably knew is what would happen, but it came as quite a shock nonetheless. Though I am busy eighteen hours a day (not to mention the miles I cover in sleep), I get little, if anything, done. If I took away the neurotic motivations and expressions, there would be little left but a few skips of my heartbeat, and maybe a smile or a sigh here and there.

School is, of course, ambiguous. I learn from interest but not from need, (making the best of my situation, so to speak). I shun almost any contact with people, partially because I have had no real encounters, and any attempt to instigate one has only left me bruised; partially because I am intensely self-conscious; but also because I am very critical of others right now, and it seems the only way I can pay respect to the people around me is to ignore them—else I just cause them pain and frustration.

I seem immersed in anger. I float around in these fantastic scenarios, punching people and screaming and yelling and imagining ridiculous acts of violence. So I tread softly.

School and study take an awful amount of discipline, concentration, force. My brain is slow and clumsy; it seems to shut down in deference to feelings, which are usually ungraceful expressions of fear, panic, frustration.

My solace and my inspiration are found in my search for beauty, which may sound trite and sentimental. But to sit by the sea at night, or walk through a fog-shrouded redwood forest leaves such a sweet taste in my mouth. A lot of my beauty is fantasy, too. Games I play with my imagination. I don't know if this is healthy or not, but it helps calm me and warms me when I'm chilled and alone.

I really wish I was in Primal Therapy like Tom is right now. I grow tired of these empty games; I don't even know the rules of most of them anyway. And time keeps on passing me by.

We are born with so much and we die with so little (if anything) left. At twenty-four I feel like I've spent my life's allowance, in haste and in waste. Horrible waste. We drive the wrong way down one-way streets, for "fear of arriving."

A big hug,
Paul

Hi -

A frantic time here: trying to finish cutting firewood, installing the winter shutters etc. before leaving for Denver day after tomorrow. Despite the opportunity to see Leslie and a few other loved ones, I dread going to the city. I'll be glad to be back and preparing for my visit to you.

I've had some hard times lately—a few good ones, too. I think it'll be therapeutic to be with you; it's really a big event for me. See you in three weeks or so.

Love,
Dad

A truly inspiring day. A trip to Big Sur, a seat in the sand and sea, alone with my thoughts and memories and the roar of the surf. Letters and calls from three old and dear friends. A moonlit sea—sparkling and serene, and most of all, a new and very powerful woman, such sweetness.

This is really food for thought. It reinforces, and actualizes, all my ideas about waiting, until the time is right and the situation presents itself. Of course I am clumsy at it, jumping at the wrong situations, or nearly missing the right ones. But tonight I connected. It seemed so easy.

A lovely young lady, delicate and fresh, like so many women I see and seek every day. But also so different. Her mind is so much like mine—her needs and aspirations, her doubts. If she were male, we could be best friends. As is, she scares me. Her youthfulness is a barrier. Though perhaps it serves the same purpose as masculiness might, foregoing sexual connotation for the more important, and exquisitely more rare, touching of mind and spirit.

Of course the sexuality is there though. She is a beautiful young girl: intense, articulate, passionate. And I see the attraction in her eyes, the excitement. I cannot focus on this, though. Nor can I purposefully avoid it. But I cannot allow this encounter to go unheeded, because of ego, fear or doubt. I must pursue it as clearly as possible, because an important connection has been made.

Life assumes more value; my lonely search has been given a gift of assurance. I feel a vitalness astir within. It is awesome.

. . . .

Hello!

Here sits I in my customary 5:00ish pose. Snuggled in the grasses just below the lip of the cliffs that run the perimeter of the seaside. Out of sight of the passersby, and out of reach of the noise of traffic and roller skaters and such that promenade along the ocean front.

From here I can see the sun sizzle into the water, I can see the birds skimming along the waves or diving from the sky straight down into the water and out again with a silvery streak of anchovy in their bills. Forty or fifty yards out is a large, lone seal, who has caught himself a sunfish and is tossing it in the air and slapping it back and forth on the water. Across the bay, Monterey Peninsula floats like a seductive mirage, on a long narrow streak of purple and red fog, that will soon encompass the beach and, later in the night, go sweeping through the deserted streets, enveloping everyone in their sleep.

I always seem to have a space in my day about now, so I always come to sit and watch the sunset. Today is cloudy, so it will be especially dramatic. It's a funny phenomenon. As soon as the sun gets within a few inches of the water, all human activity stops. All the strollers stop and look, housewives in their kitchens stop dinner preparations and come out to the front porches, cars pull over, and for ten minutes there is a profound silence and peace, and a subtle sense of comradeship amongst the beholders. Then, as soon as the last traces of red are gone, all the engines rev up and the pots and pans clatter and conversations begin anew. But for a short while, time stands still.

Things go fairly well with yours truly. In terms of common ground between us, I have realized a few long-forgotten choices, and am very meekly, though nonetheless, pursuing the breathtaking experience of some "unrestrained emotion."

Sometimes I fear that my need has juxtaposed with the first likely solution at hand, (as a young gosling will imprint on a zookeeper) but for the most part I can trust my feelings in the matter as real. Thus my emotive decisions have priority, and my poor intellect is left with the responsibility of picking up the pieces afterwards, or making amends when necessary.

A prime example happened yesterday, trivial but obvious.

I have a philosophy class that has been causing me ridiculous anguish and discomfort. But I have tried hard to keep up with it, though it's meant long nights of reading and rereading and rereading again—texts, research for papers, etc. And, though meaningless, I looked upon it as an exercise in discipline, concentration, training in withstanding bullshit.

So yesterday I went to class and, unable to make head or tails of what was going on, (mind you, this is Philosophy 1, for nitwits and freshmen) I began observing and pinpointing my anxiety. Sleepiness, numbness in my arms and legs, pounding heart, constricted throat, tense tummy, an almost insuppressible urge to run screaming out of the room (or through the window). So of course I very satisfyingly made the obvious decision that enough was enough. I sat till the end of the class, because I wanted to get an essay back that I'd spent one long weekend agonizing over. So I read the fucking thing, just for fun, and it sounds just like these ridiculous lectures and textbooks. An incredible barrage of words and phrases and clichés and definitions, and I can't make any sense out of it—and *I wrote it!* But, to top it off, at the end is the critique of the professor, praising the brilliant cohesion of my ideas, the profound insight, etc., etc.

Oh, such confusion. Maybe I really had something and just didn't know it. But I listened to my body and not my poor head, and dropped the class, and feel much better: calmer, more deliberate.

Still, this is preschool compared to the decisions to come, if I continue in this light, and I can feel those decisions, the burden of their responsibility, lurking out there on the fringes. My sleep is heavy and drugged, my eyesight blurry, my thoughts and tongue befuddled. Every encounter is tender and raw. But the choice is there. Not decided, but recognized.

Here goes the sun. I must stop and watch.

Love,
Paul

· · · · · · ·

Having a hard time with time. I figure I'll boycott old age, stabilize things here at twenty-four for a few centuries, till I learn how to backtrack, then I think I'll just grow young, like Merlin, maybe hang out at three or four for a while, and then just crawl on back into the womb and act like nothing has happened. Just another anonymous misplaced ejaculation, overt ovulation.

· · · · · · ·

I'm beginning to understand that "unrestrained expression" is a choice. The motivation or directing force for my actions has been taken over by my *feelings*; I am letting myself respond from a gut level. Any questions posed by my intellect are after the fact. My *thinking* is relegated to assume responsibility, sometimes justify, sometimes pick up the pieces left by my actions.

In doing so, I feel a trace of clarity shining through. I have felt, myself, what it feels like to be honest to that self, and how to give that gift of myself to another.

Bit by bit I am beginning to eliminate the neurotic barnacles that cling to me. My actions become precise, priorities become more obvious, tasks take on more meaning (or are less obscured by the more meaningless).

Still, I am only teasingly playing with it. I can feel, lurking out there, in here, some of the magnitude of the decisions I am going to be confronted with. And the incredible burden of responsibility which will accompany them, the anguish of the sacrifices to be made.

I only hope that my *true* strength and courage will respond in kind, and grow accordingly. I'm going to need it (close hauled). My constant and sometimes seemingly frivolous little excursions to the seaside, or into small groves of trees, out in a heavy cold wind, or a dark foggy night full of sounds—these are very important to me. On the one hand, they are an always available reminder of wonder, an easy and pure expression of beauty and of nature's other emotions. They are good medicine for anxious, cluttered living. But, more personally, they set a much needed foundation for my overwrought search for reality. The objective world has never been doubted by me; the touch of man somehow lays endless dimensions of fantasy and surrealism upon anything within its grasp!

But, the natural world is never affected. And it easily penetrates my thoughts, touching me deeply and reassuring me of my own personal goals. It lets me feel my strengths, my tools for overcoming the multitude of my fears. It passes no judgment, and expects none. It is an ever-available companion. It listens when I speak, and it coaches when I falter.

Everything that I need for myself I may find in the world of nature. My destruction lies in the world of man.

Where do I fit in?

· · · · · · ·

Standing on the shore,
staring out across the sea
beneath a silver sky
of misty, mystic paleness.
The moon hangs like a jewel,

nestled in velvet and faintly glowing.
No color save that of the silver sea and sky,
the white of moonglow and seafoam,
and black birds chasing their shadows
across the shimmering surface of silken sea.
Like opaque thoughts skimming a translucent mind.
Nothing sings so pure
as this quicksilver sea,
rising and falling
without lull or climax,
the song of the always almost,
the song of searching.

. . . .

Not sure why this comes to mind right now, but, here's an exercise in values, in priorities: define the ideal mate, lover, mainsqueeze.

Physically is easiest, though probably least important, most whimsical. A slim girl, broad of shoulder, soft rounded belly, matched by an equally soft rounded butt, fingers on the short side, but not pudgy. Breasts full and slightly pouty, with large rich nipples, lips also full and slightly pouty. Hair long and thick; any color will do, but dark and red have precedence. A smoothly modeled face, somewhat delicate. Eyes large, deep, penetrating. Skin soft, brown tones with peachy highlights. Long slender legs, strong yet soft.

An assertive woman, not too assured, but vital and spunky. Warm and yielding like Renoir's, very sensitive to soft caressing touch. Somewhat silly, impulsive but not intimidatingly so. Adventurous, talkative, moody, mysterious, gentle. Creative in action and thought. Articulate but not intellectual. Wild but sensitive like a young Arabian steed.

Ah, but my mind does wander, sometimes. . .

My visit to Paul in his new California setting was most rewarding to me, and, I trust, to him also. I found him the same person I'd been seeing reflected in his letters: excited but scared; competent but groping. It was Thanksgiving time, and his schedule allowed for many relaxed and rewarding times together: touring the lovely UCSC campus, exploring Santa Cruz's mall with its fascinating shops and street musicians, sampling local sea food, walking together through the redwoods. Then I returned to my secluded home in the forest.

. . . .

Dear Paul,

It sure feels good to be home—listening to your recording of Oscar Peterson and Joe Pass on my own stereo. Had a long soak in my big tub, then a fine lamb shank dinner. I love it here.

But the trip was awfully good for me—the time alone, the change of scenery. Mostly, though, it was good to be with you, to see your setting. Thanks for all the super times. I guess it was the best vacation I've ever had.

I certainly can see what a misfit in society I've become, during a trip like this. I belong here, and with very few people around. Wonder what I'll be like ten years from now?

As I told you on the phone tonight, I got home around noon; 2,350 miles, I figure. Some particularly peaceful times, and beautiful sights on the way home. Now I feel like I need to get reacquainted with this place. It was great, my friend. I feel closer to you than ever before. Come and see us here, soon.

Love,
Dad

A pale winter sun hangs shrouded like a jewel in silken cloth, drifting above the full, yet soft, emotion of the winter sea. The breeze and surf and bird-cries lull the mind into a warm and fluid reverie, a stillness like a womb, encasing all things.

A young man sits in the sand, unmoving, watching little birds wading in the foam at the edges of the sea, the feelings behind his eyes rising and falling like the swell of the waves, yet never quite breaking into tangible thoughts. Sensing that beyond all fears and doubtful indecision, beyond despair and cold confusion, his dreams are true, and his reality becomes known through the love and trust he shares with a few special people.

. . . .

Hello Papa,

Christmas morning finds me lounging on my bench by the sea. Its rhythmic turbulence and its luminous, opaque satin surface seem to echo the rhythmic patterns in the grey batik of the sky. The sound of the waves could easily be the sound of the breezes to a blind man, or a childish man.

It's warm and peaceful today. I feel a glow deep in my gut, a soft, complacent, post-orgasmic type of glow. A rare treat indeed. Too often I panickedly dart to and fro like some frantic fly trapped in a glass house. Either I'm soaring to exhilarating heights on the wax wings of my oh-so-potent fantasies, or I'm groveling around in the overgrown forest of my psyche, digging holes in its rich, putrid soil. Never far from digging that ultimate hole, climbing in and pulling it in after me.

The thought of death is constantly lurking in the wings, peering at me from the periphery of my mind, waiting for its cue like some grandiose curtain call on closing night.

The last few months in Durango were closer than they've ever been. I had the plan, I had the tools, I certainly as shit had the pain. Always egging me on for one more day was the commitment I had to design and build that rocking chair for my dear friend Weston. Then I came here expecting to outrun those shadows. And now when the thought of death oozes out of the quagmire, I think of the little one that is inside Leslie's belly, and somehow I feel an awesome responsibility to him/her, knowing of the vicarious influence that I hold.

California and I don't seem to be getting along. I had a fairly good idea of what it was like here, of what I was up against, but I thought I could hold my own—my piercing Colorado spirit shining like a ruby in this social septic tank of stagnant humanity.

But it's beginning to wear me out. I feel like a fly in a hurricane, trying to beat it upwind to some unknown goal, around and around and around. Trying to be true to the little bit of truth in me, I don't feel equipped to play this California Super Bowl. They don't make football suits for butterflies.

"Dear Santa, thanks for the wonderful suntan and all these women and acres of freedom—but what I really wanted was just a little strength. Perhaps if you've kept the sales receipts . . ."

Oh well, complaining is nothing more than sloppy verbal masturbation; there's no substitute for the real thing.

Paul

Dear Paul,

Your Christmas letter was very painful to read, but I'm glad you can share some of your insides with me. Today was a peaceful day for me. Mostly I've felt pretty good since I got back here, not pressing too hard with my projects. But the last few days I worked pretty continuously (redoing the skylight seals) so today I took a walk, listened to Oscar Peterson, baked a little bread, and lit our new Scandia woodstove for the first time. It's going to be a good one.

A month ago I was there. Those several days we had together made an unusual mark on me. I remember it all with exceptional clarity and fondness; glad I came, and I look forward to having you here.

A very atypical January, I think. The ground is dry—the air balmy. Lots of birds are still around. And I see many elk tracks, but no critters.

Forgot to tell you: the seafood I bought on the wharf was delightful; provided us with six or eight terrific dinners: crab Newburg, baked cod, etc. It all made the return trip fine, as did the little terrarium—a Christmas gift. At Kayenta, on the Arizona reservation, I found five excellent books on Navajo rug weaving, so my Christmas shopping was about finished when I got home.

I think of you very often indeed, and hope things are going good for you at least part of the time.

Love,
Dad

Hi,

Just got your letter; they always seem to come on those strange shades-of-grey days, void of personality and totally vulnerable to any outside power. Really kind of a pleasant feeling; changes occur more easily, a lack of resistance makes for easier transitions and realizations, and words from you are always extra inspiring, which is all I could ever ask for.

The past week has been really pretty nice. I've made some new and very special friends. I spent a couple of days with Andy, the one man I now have contact with that I can feel totally at ease with. Some very good friends from Durango popped in; more than just a few chance encounters are beginning to hint at some special meanings. Loneliness has been pre-empted for a while, and I have a chance to stop and catch my breath—step outside and look myself over a bit. Life becomes richer, emptiness but a memory; every day brings new inspiration and a little more clarity.

Tonight I feel good here in Santa Cruz. Life is a wonderful gift, the future looks bright and exciting; I feel strength welling up from deep inside.

How different every day is from the last one, and I along with it. I hope I never stop being surprised. How I wish we could take a hike up our favorite hill together, feel the breeze, listen to the birds sing. . . Perhaps that time is not too far away.

Paul

Dear Paul,

Got your last letter; you were having a good day. I have some of both kinds, but I seem to keep making progress. Lots of good time alone, frequently out in the woods—sometimes four or five hours, or sometimes just for lunch if I'm busy. The projects now are mostly interior, in the nature of decorating, so my efforts usually show very visible results and the house exhibits more and more of its final character. Very satisfying.

Still virtually no snow during all of December and January. Two years ago we received nearly one hundred inches each of those months! And always warm and sunny. We have disabled our (expensive) electric furnace and are totally and comfortably heated solarly.

Life is about the same for me; my biggest preoccupation is with the number and variety of things that, so often, still frighten me—at a deep level. Wisdom comes hard.

Love,
Dad

Papa,

I guess it's the little boy in me speaking when I address you as papa. That's surely how I feel today. So many times in the past few days I've wanted to call you, but it's not words that I need. When I speak to you in my mind it brings tears trickling, filling my head and squeezing out my eyes like some rain-saturated leaky roof, swollen and bloated.

It's been so grey, greyer than words or thoughts—the sky and sea so stormy and loud and awesomely powerful, I cannot tell if they are but some Cartesian projection of my frantic mind, exploding.

Reality fades in the heavy shrouds of fog that blanket my will. Search as I may, I find only tiny bits and pieces of it, like irritating cracker crumbs in my bed that keep me awake and thinking, when all I want is to submerge myself in soulful dream. Still, it's a small step from dream to nightmare.

Something in my life has gone awry. It's funny, I know it is inside of me; yet it is so much more powerful than I. More powerful than fear, than need or want, touch or hope, thoughts or imagination. I've used up all my tricks for combating the unknown. All I can do is let go to it, and trust in its benevolence.

Worries and empty responsibilities; how I wish I could take a quiet walk with you up Chris Mountain, watch the clouds and listen to the trees and feel the breezes tickle my imagination . . .

Send me some lichen and some bluejay shit and an old cucumber stem from the compost pile, a snowflake and a cat whisker and a blue molecule of dry mountain air, some sawdust from the garage, a pine needle or two—throw in a hug; that's all I really need. It's life and life only.

Paul

Paul,

Such painfully beautiful words you send me: expressive of your very insides. I probe and search my soul for something valid, something help-ful to tell you, but am brought up short, very quickly, against my own limitations and confusions.

I can find, from my own poor understandings, nothing wrong with

*you, nothing to suggest that you try to change. (Perhaps you're simply
too much like me.) I do find, instead, multitudes of failings in our
society, its expectations and its habits. It is a most baffling life we're
called upon to live.*

*I have no explanations. I have only compassion and love for you—
and hope and confidence that it will truly work itself into a solution—
will be worth all you've put into it over so many years.*

More words fail me.

> *Inadequately,*
> *Dad*

Hello,

If I can fill up the huge amount of blank space on this beautiful
Japanese card with this little pen, I fear your eyes may suffer a grave
misjustice. Certainly my thoughts will run out long before ink or
empty page, not to mention my patience at trying to keep my hand
from smearing the words in excited left-handedness.

This card is very reflective of my mind. If I could have painted it,
words would be unnecessary. There is a vague numinosity to the
world. Not so much a grey haze, but a richer silver and gold one that
surrounds me—not so much as a fog, but as a powerful projection of
my psyche.

Flowers blossom, brittle leaves fall from trees; I can see this all
around me in my objective world, too. It is striking to see a crimson
maple tree dropping dry leaves, adjacent to a blossoming apple tree,
dropping velvet petals.

There is a subtle yet intense life in the foreground, the quiet
interchange of birds at rest. And yet the true power is in the inference
of the vast expanses of depth that recede into the background. Grasses
sprout from dead stumps. It's really a peace of someone's mind. How
rich and awesome must life have been four hundred years ago. Void
of clutter, empty responsibilities, seductive rationale and the deaf-
ening roar of consciousness.

My confusion and instability at this time, in spite of my awareness that I am a capable person, seem to be an unconscious yet deliberate act of my own. With the still uncertain acknowledgment of my

inner strength and its ultimate integrity, and my clumsy attempts at giving it free rein as the motivator of my life, I seem to purposefully bungle my ability to organize my material life: school, jobs, money, future, relationships. Knowing myself to be basically a lazy person, if I allowed my external life to become too comfortable and easy, then like so many other people, I would simply immerse myself in pleasant habits, and any inner growth would be minimal, and probably overlooked. Thus, I force myself to walk that razor's edge; I maintain the rawness of conflict and turmoil. By keeping myself off balance, I make available that choice.

My predominant fear is of the unknown. And underlying that is a lack of confidence that causes me to question whether what I so vaguely seek is a perception, or a personal projection. Is it real? If it is not, if it is just subjective neurotic projection, then I am lost. To give myself up to that would be a life of insanity.

From whence comes the strength to overcome that fear? So that I can begin a forward motion, allow my material world to fall into place—not as a goal in itself, but as an essential means towards my more important ends. It's really frightening.

Without your assurance, and a few others', I doubtlessly would have given up long ago. What is it that causes people to reach out? Why do we help each other along?

It's a wonder-full mystery, worthy of a lifetime in pursuit of its understanding. Thanks for being you.

Me

· · · · · · ·

Hmm, what is it that draws us/me/you to write tonight? Obviously I have been more than a little affected by a lady—Marie. Why? What's the big deal?

I feel excited. I feel afraid. I feel inadequate. I wonder why women like this are attracted to me; I wonder why they are becoming apparent in my life. Firstly, they are very beautiful (applause from my ego). But more importantly, what causes the fear and confusion is that they are very full-on, very intelligent, determined, seemingly in control of their lives, not restrictively, but passionately and deliberately motivated.

Why are they drawn to me? Is there something I can learn from this? Am I playing games, acting confident and alluring, or is there something that they see that I don't? Is a part of my true nature peeking out? And can I put this to good use? Or is it just a temporary ego booster. A shaky retaining wall against the violent stormy seas of my psyche?

The same old question: perception or projection. What is real?

· · · · · · ·

Hello,

Here sits I in the kitchen drinking tea and grinning at my reflection in the glass of your seascape print—my Christmas gift, now matted and framed. Still a little punchy from a long night of sleep. I've been monitoring my dreams pretty carefully too, so I wake up five or six times during the night to see what my funny little brain is up to, and you know how befuddled you get when awoken out of a dream, not to mention five or six. Plus, it's Friday. After my regularly scheduled midweek crisis of too-much-too-soon, a four day weekend is really something to grin about.

Things are pretty nice right now. At least they're stable. Perhaps it's just the eye of my storm, but it's nice to have an emotional breather before taking off again on my roller coaster of confusion.

I've been sharing the company of a particularly fine young lady, Marie, and after just a short time together have reached a level of understanding and intimacy that is truly amazing. She seems to bring out the best in me, so to speak. I knew it was in there somewhere.

Also Matt, a friend from Durango who just moved out here, bought a twenty-eight-foot hull and is beginning to build his own sailboat. You should see his plans. What a beautiful project. I'll be closely involved in the woodwork (teak and mahogany) and am a potential candidate for crewman. Besides that, he is a very sensitive and compassionate person, and I need a good close male companion; I have felt that lacking.

My mind has been clear and I'm learning some valuable things about myself. Recognizing some strengths, and acknowledging weaknesses. I've found the world in general is not very accepting of my ideas and designs for living; I'm not practical enough for it, and I can see it is going to be some struggle to come to terms with that, while remaining true to myself.

But, on the other hand, I find people as *individuals* responding to me on a personal level in a very wonderful way, and that is where my power lies.

School is beginning to fall into place. I can see what I want from it, what it wants back, and just what sort of compromises are necessary. I'm pretty low on organizational skills though, so that takes some doing.

Me

Hi-

Here's a real mellow day, the kind that brings me thoughts of you. A gentle snow falling outside, a comforting fireplace, stuffed chicken roasting in the oven, nice little projects to work on: a good day. After I got the stuffing made and the bird in the oven, I put on Oscar Peterson and his friends and reclined in my favorite chair for a nap; Tigger climbed up on my tummy and joined me, as he frequently does.

I've gotten back into stained glass projects again, and am really enjoying it. (If there's something you'd like, tell me.) Also a little wood working here and there. But, most exciting, I'm walking around that big juniper log in the garage, mulling over shapes, and now am almost ready to draw a few tentative lines, fire up the chain saw, and carve myself a lavatory stand for my bathroom! A very inspiring job; hope it goes well.

Next big project is the two stained glass globes to hang over our kitchen stove/table island. Quite demanding, I think, so I started off with a couple of smaller glass projects to get the feel again. Also, I've changed from using lead came to copper foil—much more satisfying.

As I told you, I spend a lot of time digesting your thoughtful letters, trying to fulfill my half of the communication process so as to perceive, with some accuracy, what you were experiencing as you wrote. Often I find them very profound. It's always a special day when one arrives.

I'm still doing a lot of hiking in the woods; nearly dry out there (until today). So far only a little snow has stayed on the ground, but it looks a little more determined now, as nightfall approaches. We could use a big one.

I'm beginning to get my life more like I want it here, lately—except I'm not much into my own music, yet. It feels like the time is coming, though. Hope things are good for you.

Love,
Dad

Now I find myself becoming more involved with Marie. Young, so alive, hints of incredible depth and potential. Her mind so agile and clear. Her young body so sweet and firm and perfect. Her spirit so potent. If she knew of the power she holds over me, would she want it? How does she feel when I hold her, when I'm inside of her? How does she feel when she thinks of me throughout the day?

So easily beguiled, enchanted, entranced.

. . . .

My Tools and Weapons:
- imagination: for creative thought and a fresh attitude.
- intuitive sensitivity: access to that part of me that resonates.
- health: I know how it feels to be strong and clear.
- passion: sometimes translated as ideal expectations and motivations.
- looks: innocent, youthful, friendly, at times intriguing.
- intelligence: not an abundance of brain power, but a graceful mind.
- inspiration and support: from an infinite world of indefatigable beauty, and from many people who believe in me.
- love: constantly percolating to the surface.
- history: a very rich background of personal experience.
- humility: I've earned it.
- mortality: I understand the responsibility of that knowledge.

. . . .

Fear of attachment:
Funny, I wouldn't mind someone possessing me, but when I find

myself becoming so invested in another, it really frightens me. I guess I don't mind having power over someone, but woe, if they've power over me. I know how much pain we can cause each other.

I begin to see how much it will hurt when I lose Marie; and still, I have to give myself to her fully, stay totally committed, because I know what I stand to lose if I never try. I fear the intensity with which I want to give myself to her. She is supporting my reality right now. I give my love to her desperately, from need. I shower her with attention, trying to charm into captivity.

It's almost like a race; can I sap enough strength from her to be strong enough in time to deal with the pain and loneliness when she leaves me? When she peeks beyond my facade and finds I am but half a person? As half a person, I can only give her half of what she needs. Soon that won't be enough.

· · · · · · ·

I'm looking for a home. Somewhere to rest my feet. Somewhere I can slip out of my daily costume and into something more comfortable.

A place I can snuggle into, warm and calm, without lies and hidden fears, where all my inspirations can hang on the walls, and my unrestrained expressions can litter the floor. A place for quiet thought and raucous laughter, tears of joy and pain.

It needn't be large, but open spaces as well as cozy places are nice. I'd like a window outside my bedroom with a tree, so the birds can visit, my cat can perch, and the wind and rain can whisper to me in the night. Close to the sea so that I may hear the surf roar and so my room will be filled with clear ocean breezes.

Lots of light for my plants, and a large kitchen with a nice view, a front porch to sit on and watch the folks drift by, and a yard of grass to get naked and sun in. Some friendly neighbors around to chat with, and perhaps even a person or two inside to share with. You know the type: direct, compassionate, creative, friendly, real.

> Housed inside my surest self,
> self that is my home.
> Not mask nor mirror nor fragile shell,
> no hollow rooms —
> no empty shelves —
> no lies I cannot tell.
> The air is filled with dream and thought,
> the walls hung with inspiration,
> the floor littered with emotion,
> and my unrestrained expression.

Paul's concern over his inner anguish led him to seek the help of a local psychotherapist—hoping that it would begin to provide some relief, some glimmer of progress in his earnest—almost desperate—search for himself, for rightness. He found it slow going.

Hello,

I've a few quiet moments to sit in this warm, late afternoon calm; it seems a good time to share some thoughts.

Finals are just a couple of weeks away; there's lots of paperwork to resolve, lots of time spent getting Marie off to France—mostly making the most of our few remaining weeks together, trying to realize a bond that will hold together over thousands of miles and dozens of lonely days.

Tonight is a special celebration. We have a lull in our studies; Marie, who has been suffering from an infection, will after three long weeks, be able to drink wine, make love, eat a good fish dinner, and go dancing. Youthful decadence! Tomorrow we drive up to San Francisco; tennis with friends, visit some museums, do some shopping.

As usual, I am very up and down. Extremely sensitive right now; tears always close at hand, tremors of anxiety, like earthquakes in the night. Always on the verge of change, yet feeling as if I live on the periphery of reality, never involved, just wishing and wanting like the new kid in town, standing alone at the edge of a crowded playground, watching.

Therapy looks promising. It vents desperation anyway, and stands in my mind as a glimmer of hope, like the early morning glow on the horizon: faint, cold, but assuring.

I think of you often, both in weakness and strength—sadness and joy, but always with warmth and affection.

A big hug,
Paul

. . . .

Part of what I fear in becoming close to someone is the giving up of a part of me in the compromise of sharing. I have so little to give.

I lose my own small bit of self when I become involved with another, because I so desperately need a reality, that I cling on to theirs, and they respond positively, thinking they have found a *friend*—when what they have found is a *parasite.*

And when they are gone, I must face the pain of my emptiness. And when I am with them, I sometimes must face that emptiness too, in seeing what rich lives they have.

While I have only facade; this empty shell, with just a few dried-up kernels of goodness that rattle around inside: endless echoes which fill the hollow spaces and make them ache.

Deep in my dreams I dance,
yet weeping and weak I awaken.
Blind birds sing silent songs
outside my window.

Dear Paul,

As you have requested, here are some musings on past times which I hope will be helpful in your therapy:

I think I remember the day you were conceived: a peaceful Sunday afternoon in autumn—in the bedroom of our small rented carriage house, behind a handsome brownstone mansion on a stately street in Colorado Springs. Before you were born we scrounged a way to buy a small house in a development across town—not nearly as pleasant as the old carriage house.

But I painted up the place, built a little furniture, meanwhile invented the famous baby carriage (which I never succeeded in marketing), played organ at church, got promoted to a more demanding position at work— and in general kept moving fast enough that, like so many people, I wouldn't have time to look inside and face my real truths. I was proud to display a wife and new daughter as lovely symbols of my very orderly and on-schedule accomplishment scheme, but I never considered the importance or the opportunity of real intimacy with either of them, or with anyone else! I was totally a cold fish—but one that my acquaintances respected and admired, as I wanted them to.

Thus you were born of two immature, driven, super-respectable and responsible children, aged twenty-six and twenty-seven. We were, by the way, severely pressed financially in those years. Bought everything on time payments, borrowed money all over, stayed nervously close to the edge of bankruptcy all the time.

I remember taking time off from work the morning you began to be born—feeling that I really shouldn't be gone, and fearful about the work not getting done. When you didn't arrive as soon as expected, I called in to apologize for staying longer; they assured me it was all right. The birth itself I knew nothing of; I wasn't there, wasn't involved (fathers never were in those days). You were one of the last babies born in an antiquated wing of Penrose Hospital before it was razed for a new addition.

The obstetrician was a friend from church, and I guess we trusted him, and that the delivery went relatively smoothly.

I fixed up a pretty little room for you, just as in later years I built playhouses and treehouses, bought bicycles etc. etc.; did all the right things—except touching you, enjoying you, getting acquainted, helping you ease into life. I feel I was largely a failure as a father in those days. I had a lot to hearn about being a husband, too.

*I think that most of the limited time and energy I gave you were directed at making sure you did what you **should** do: learned discipline, got good grades, suffered through little league, played piano. Always you and Leslie were beautifully dressed and groomed.*

Do you remember remedial sessions at Phillips Grade School for dealing with some sort of speech difficulty? Then I also hired a psychologist to evaluate you and Les—to help me make certain you were progressing properly—on the road to accomplishment, I suppose.

There were a few vacation trips that, it seems to me, were relatively relaxing for us. And I remember Sunday evenings, when we'd fix a big plate of snacks for supper and watch "Bonanza" together. I recall very few other peaceful times; I rarely felt peace myself, then, I know.

The presence of the grandparents, with all the shit we endured at Christmas, birthdays etc. was exasperating to me, and possibly damaging to you. I don't know how much of that you recall; I could possibly fill in around your memory if you wish.

*You have asked only about your early times—not those years closer to the separation and divorce. Although some of that is very painful for me to contemplate, I will discuss those times with you, if you think it would be useful. One more observation: in searching out elements of our past, the memories to be most trusted, in my opinion, are the **first person** ones—not second person. If I recall a baby in a mother's arms, as seen from across a room, it probably was not me. If I experience the feel of mother's skin, the sound of her breathing, her smell, or other more nebulous sensations, up very close—I trust those as mine.*

Well, enough for now. I am eager to help you in this voyage into yourself—you need only ask. I think about you often, and long to see you.

Hopefully,
Dad

· · · · · · ·

As always, I hoped fervently that these words of mine were the right ones—that they would prove to be of real help. And yet, I usually was left with a gnawing feeling of helplessness—of insufficiency.

Dad,

Hello. It seems like months since I've written, not so much from lack of time but lack, or maybe exhaustion, of creative expression. School has really got me hopping. Writing lots of poetry, painting, sculpting, reading poetry, sailing, tennis; I'm even taking a class in female gynecology and physiology. I need the science credit to graduate, and it seemed inside information on women might come in handy.

I learn more from the experience of class than I do from the subject matter. It's the largest class on campus, about 450 people, and less than a dozen are men. Believe me, it is an awesome feeling to be surrounded and outnumbered by that many women. Talking about sexuality, no less. It is always just barely short of a riot. These women are really angry. Any mention of men brings on booing and hissing and foot stamping.

Do you have life insurance for my being torn to shreds by a mob of hysterical feminists? If I ever disappear . . .

A big hug,
Paul

Dear Paul,

I'm out in the woods alone today—north of the old Butcher homestead, east of Chris Mountain. A superb spring day. The billowy clouds could bring showers (been a drop or two through the sunshine) but I brought my poncho. Wish I could have shared my lunch with you: salad of alfalfa sprouts, lettuce, celery, white cheddar, dates, fresh-roasted sesame seeds—and honey/mayonnaise dressing! I often think of our lunch together that day we drove the truck to the ranger station and walked down to Devil Creek. Some exquisite times we've had together.

I brought your letter and photo out with me today. Undoubtedly the most handsome portrait of you I've ever seen—but very hard for me to look at. You were looking into the camera, and the feeling I get is that you've just come from a therapy session of screaming at your father (deservedly so) for all he did to you in your early life. Painful. What can you tell me of the setting and background of that photo? Did you feel you were looking at me?

Mostly, I'm having good and peaceful times. Still spending no appreciable time at the piano, but I feel I'm close to starting. The status of the greenhouse, garden work, various projects, my own insides—everything that bears upon really getting into music—is coming into place.

Oh, I forgot the biggest news: last night, with my Chicken Alfredo, I served, for dinner, our very first home-grown green-house artichoke. In Colorado! Absolutely perfect, and at least eight more coming along on the same plant. We're delighted.

The joint plans for the distinctive little cradle to be created for Leslie's coming baby are getting very exciting; I love these projects shared with you. Write when you feel like it; call when you can afford it; and let me know how I can help with the cradle.

Love,
Dad

It's been a while. It's usually pain that prompts me to write, it seems: pain and question. I try to be stoic, strong and detached—understanding and assured—agreeable. But what I really want sometimes is to scream and rage and beat my head against the wall.

With all my confusion, though, my efforts eventually seem to be paying off—slowly. I feel reassured that through all these years of struggle, I have managed to maintain my uniqueness and individuality intact, and it is beginning to express itself, and to gain in strength.

· · · · · · ·

Hello,

Here I sit at a time- and hand-worn table on the patio of the Big Sur Inn. We stopped here and had coffee and fresh pie, remember?

I'm here for a few days, maybe hiding, maybe running. I huddle here in this damp cold fog of loneliness, trying to keep my few small coals of self aglow, like some lost wanderer in a storm.

I stay in the Little Room, next to van Gogh's Bedroom and down the hall from Petite Cuisine. There's no lock on the door; drawings done by past wayfarers hang askew on the old barnwood walls. White and purple morning glories peek in my window; cats copulate outside my door. I love it here.

It smells just like the lodge at Clark, Colorado, and brings back warm and touching feelings from that period of my adolescence when I felt that I was real. My summers in the mountains were like exotic dreams, and the memory of that fills my friendly Little Room with placid warmth.

Today I climbed down the cliffs to where we saw that large herd of seals. A few dozen were lounging around, and I was able to get within fifteen feet or so of them. Tonight I'll go to Esalen, a little retreat down the coast, open from one to five in the morning, with hot-tubs and saunas that sit right on the edge of the cliffs, overlooking the sea. Tonight the moon is full, so if the fog clears it will be lovely. If only I had a few weeks, it seems my head would finally clear. Just a day or two at a time seems such a tease. Vacation days should always outnumber days of strife.

Well, my stomach says dinner. I've some fresh bread and French cheese and fresh fruits I bought along the way; a small carafe of wine so I can eat and drink in my room. Breakfast was oats with fresh strawberries and cream, served by the fire on old-world china with a bouquet of morning flowers to garnish the plate. A nice way to begin a cloudy, fog-enveloped day.

Me

Hello-

Wish we were together for your birthday; I'd cook up something scrumptious, have a little wine, a little music, and some good talk. You're in my thoughts a lot. I picture you sitting above the surf, or working behind the oyster bar, or sweating and trembling under the covers at midday wondering what it's all about. You tell me often that you don't seem to have established much of a direction. It's my feeling that, despite all the painful confusion, you have uncommonly good command of many

of life's truly important concepts and accomplishments (not always the most readily visible ones). And you're my best and closest friend. I sure look forward to seeing you.

Just had lunch and a nap before I started this letter— out between the Butcher homestead and Butcher spring where I wrote you once before. A gorgeous day, and such moist green surroundings, like the Muir Woods, almost. Nearly daily showers lately. Our outdoor garden is lush already; greenhouse even more so. And so many birds this year. I've really tuned into bird sounds this spring.

I brought your picture, some recent letters, and the group of your latest poems with me today. Found the poetry very impressive and touching, more so on each rereading. In some ways we seem able to exchange more intimacies in our writings than we can face-to-face. Why is that?

I received new band-saw blades in the mail the other day, so now I can finish the staves for Les's cradle, and be ready for final assembly when you return the ends with your marquetry applied. I'm eager to get it together and do the final shaping and finishing. What a fine joint project!

I have a modest (meaning cheap) birthday gift picked out for you, but haven't been able to obtain it yet; I'll keep trying.

Think I'll pack up and head home. Happy Birthday, and

Love,

Dad

Faith, Fond Memory, and Friendship
The Twenty-sixth Year

Dad,

I sit here in the cool shade of a large grove of redwoods. They surround me in a comfy circle. Looking straight up is a sphere of blue sky, like a giant telescope; each cloud or bird which passes by is magnified in its solitude, its singularity.

Through the trunks to the east I see a sensuous hill of golden grass, scattered with receding groves of redwood and eucalyptus. To the west is the sea, miles off and bordered with its perpetual silver lining of hazy fog.

I'm staying temporarily fifteen miles north of Santa Cruz with Matt, who lives in a big barn nestled in the quiet. Like your house, it is a haven of serenity and a sanctuary for the pensive and complacent. A rest home for weary souls tired of battling the indomitable forces of confusion and undirected passion. I am glad to be done with the setting on Dufour Street, but am vulnerable in my homelessness.

I live my life now on faith, fond memory, and friendship. Especially friendship. If it weren't for the love and tender response from you, Leslie, and several others, I could not survive. Lost in the hugeness of myself, I would disappear if left alone, without the reminder from others that I am worthy to exist, to take up space and breathe precious air. My life is so precarious, yet so valuable because it is so delicate. It's a wonder I have survived.

Your letter was beautiful. No finer birthday gift could have been given. I needed your assurance badly on a day which magnified my feelings and doubts and misgivings on being alive. So little I've to show for twenty-five years of hard work, so little to build on for the next twenty-five. I feel feeble and weary. I am frightened beyond words. Still, I struggle on. Toward what? I ask myself daily, hourly. From what?

Love,
Paul

And, scrawled on a birthday card to me:

Dad,

Lying here on a quiet beach, naked to the sun. Giant waves roll in, so big they look in slow motion, and funnel in to this tiny cove, building speed and rushing up the beach, stopping a few yards from my feet. A brisk breeze blows the foam from the crest of the waves, and the sky is filled with a thin gauze of fog, staining it white, and very fresh.

I lie here straining to find the peace and clarity of mind with which to describe, convince, assure you what a fine and beautiful man you are. But all I am able to do is to simply thank you for being who you are; you have made my life so much richer. That is all my feeble words can do. I hope in action someday I may return the compliment and the inspiration. It is worth the pain of this silly life to have your friendship.

Love,
Paul

Dear Paul,

You find me today in an unusual setting (for me): lunch, alone, at the Pagosa Lodge; I'm spending most of the day alone. Must have been a month since I've been in town; I venture out less and less frequently. Seems I enjoy it more (both when at home and away) that way.

101

The little note you sent with my birthday card moved me deeply. Possibly the most direct and succinct expressions you've made to me. I'm almost glad you couldn't find additional words.

I just paused for a while and reflected upon what a strange and tortuous path it was that led us into this ultimately close and wonderful relationship. Life is indeed curious—and seldom logical. Whatever that word really means.

Our joint efforts on Leslie's cradle were consummated in a piece of exceptional grace and beauty (by my perception) and most happily received, as you know. It would feel good to try something else together sometime. It seems to go very smoothly for us.

Adios for now. I love you.

Dad

Midafternoon, after a long wait, of
wonder, and fear, and half ripened reality,
Leslie and Rob together create a young girl child.
Allison.
This is truly beyond my comprehension.
Like a dream.
It breaks the hard-edged callous of my pain,
for a moment;
I cry,
with happiness.
With the happiness of life.
This happiness of life,
it is beyond me.
It is beyond me?

· · · · · · ·

Dad,

Here sits I behind the oyster bar late at night; close to closing time. The predominant feeling I get is of being out of my element, having to adapt, to compromise, in order to deal with my situation in the way which is expected. I wonder if I'll ever feel differently. Only in the woods have I ever felt at home—and perhaps lying in my woman's arms late at night or early in the morning. Must I spend my whole life seeking myself, pursuing definition, piecing myself together bit by bit? What will I do when I find it, when all the little blocks are stacked up? Turn and run? Knock it down? Will I recognize it? What would it feel like if I had that definition right now? I think I would be immensely powerful.

Home now. Safely in bed, enveloped in moonlight filtered through a warm ocean fog. Weary from the weariness that only comes from the effort of trying to suck meaning from a meaningless task. Dammit dad, you didn't ask me if I wanted to be born. Now you tease me with false promise. How much easier it would be if you, too, hated me. Now, I'm stuck in the middle. Too weak to live, too weak to die. Something is terribly wrong, and keeps getting worse. With always just the faintest glint of hope to taunt me into trying one more day, one more hour, one more goddam minute.

It's all up to chance now. I have no answers.

I must sleep now. Thank god for sleep.

Paul

Dear Paul,

I've been mulling on some things I'd like to pass on; perhaps there's something helpful here.

It isn't sick, it isn't insane to yearn and search for a right feeling, a natural feeling inside as we live our lives and experience our surroundings, our relationships, our work. Rather the civilized world is sick when it pressures us to violate those inner promptings and to force-fit ourselves into accepted forms. The "civilized" world with its Wall Street Journal, CDs and RVs, Mastercards, jet set, Department of Defense, and several trillion other everyday inanities.

Myself, I think it likely that present-day humanity is so alien to the normal natural earth, that the earth will, before long, reject man totally—then promptly heal itself of man's damages. So that in a short time—perhaps a few thousand or a few million years—there will be no evidence left of Homo Sapiens and his struggles.

Meanwhile, the social system is very intolerant of those who don't readily acquiesce to its ways. This puts us in a bind: we are ill-equipped for a really natural life, our predecessors having gradually abandoned the ways, the skills necessary for that; but we are incapable of adapting quickly and smoothly enough to the changing demands of the technologic/economic systems ruling us, to exist peacefully within them, either. To those of us who can still feel, it can be extremely painful.

Can it be a good life, in any real sense of the word? Maybe, but it seems to me to require a massive personal adjustment to (1) get our insides healthy, and (2) get away from much of the tragic system. At least that's my way; perhaps others have found different ways.

I've been rereading some of your recent stuff—particularly the poems of early April. I am astounded at the beauty and insight contained in those few words. You really have a lot going for you. Then your reflecting on your birthday "so little I've to show for twenty-five years of hard work, so little to build on for the next twenty-five." I ask myself how much better off was I at twenty-five than you, in the things that matter to me now. Answer: not better—worse; much worse.

Sometimes I fear that some of the things I say to you may be taken as just positive thinking: comfortable bullshit to buck you up when you're down. I'm incapable of that. The things I choose to tell you are real to me, and deeply held. And probably more revealing of me than I've ever been to anyone else. I hope that they are not clever, but true; not impressive, but helpful.

I think of you every day.

> *Love,*
> *Dad*

Dad,

Late at night; the honeymoon suite—Deetjen's Big Sur Inn. No different than the other rooms here except it's got a fireplace, a lock on the door, a private courtyard in the garden, and the bed doesn't squeak.

I sit before the Franklin stove; calm, sleepy, warm, sated after a fine dinner of roast chicken, and a dessert of sweet, carefree, quiet sex.

Marie lies in bed asleep, but I am restless. Not anxious, just awake. Life is profound, and I am not ready to let go of my wonder. Life alone is amazing; life in love is ludicrous beyond my feeble powers to comprehend.

The situation with Marie goes incredibly well. It was very awkward at first, but she, with her gentle, powerful directness, eased right on through my fear, and now, after three days of foggy Big Sur, quiet walks, lovemaking and talk, we are every bit as close, and more, than when she left for Europe. She is a woman of extraordinary personal power which, in my stronger moments, is very inspiring; at other times it is intimidating, making me feel feeble and helpless. But of course, she cannot make me feel anything I haven't already got inside, so the important thing is the intensity of my feelings when I am with her.

It feels very good to have my love awakened and accepted. My life of late has left me hard and calloused, almost bitter, and Marie has reversed that and succeeded in initiating once again the process of softening. I do not mind being vulnerable to her. If only the rest of the world saw me as she seems to, as you seem to, I would have no need for fear.

That makes it very tempting to encompass myself in a little safe world of Marie, but luckily I can see that she would not tolerate that at all; her independence is awesome, and it keeps me from clutching and clinging.

I don't know, Dad. As much as I detest expectation now, and see the futility of living off other people's energy, I can't help but wonder if perhaps this beautiful woman might just provide the incentive I need to finally commit myself to living life. I cannot dangle in limbo forever. Without change comes death. I still don't know which it will be. However, I can see both sides now. I have only to decide.

Of course.

I love you,
Paul

Dear Paul,

Yes, love is a perpetual wonderment. I'm delighted you've found what and whom you have found. As you are so aware, my own rocky road of experience with mates, with women, has not been much of a model—still isn't. (Sometimes I wonder just where my marriage is going.) But, along the way, it sure brings a large measure of marvelous rewards. Nothing in our lives quite like it; even my deep feelings for so many different musical experiences are not the equal of the impact of love. Lovely love!

The miracle of Allison's birth is very much with me these last weeks. They seem well, all of them. My biggest feeling for the whole episode is "Leslie isn't little anymore." Me—a grandfather??

Curiously,
Dad

Dad,

Riding home from work, late at night, with only the fog-filtered starlight to guide my way through the inky corridor of trees. I am befuddled by too much wine, noise, and the confusion of resistance. I wince as my stomach and back agonize over each ripple in this steep, narrow road. These days my body feels the pain my heart will not.

After a while, the silence of the night, the cool air, and the exertion clear my mind, I arrive home somewhat quiet, somewhat safe. The lights of Monterey sparkle across the bay. Dogs howl and doves mourn.

I have been learning a lot lately. It all boils down to how naive I am. What to do with such knowledge? If I could find a way to use it in a positively deliberate fashion, it would become wisdom.

Now, though, all I have is myself.

Here are photos of the hardwood jewelry box I just finished. Keep them as long as you like. I can go to Marie's if I want to see what it looks like. And, I'll use any excuse to be with her. She's really a jewel among the rest of this rat shit of humanity.

So are you!

Paul

Despite the optimism and reinforcement which Marie provided for Paul (and, oddly, also as an indirect result of it) he found himself on a path of worsening confusion and despair, as he puzzled over how he could be so happy, and at the same time, so troubled. He wondered naggingly what was wrong inside him, or was anything wrong, and how could he find out; what should he do to try to fix it? And on and on endlessly. He confided some of these painful feelings to his journal, and some to me in his letters.

After days of leisure and pleasure, seeming serenity and clarity, my body gives out, refusing food and exercise. My mind rejects any patterns of thought, my heart won't accept any love.

The energy gained from Marie wanes; my usual feelings of overwhelming fear and instability, smallness and inadequacy, despair, anxiety, fatigue and surrender, set in. Intimidated by Marie's spirit and vitality, realizing how much more I have at stake than she, I foolishly make her the focus of my life, while I remain but a part of hers. Her approach is so much more healthy.

So, knowing this, I must respect her independence, and smother my own desperate need, weaning myself from her company, making sure that I give, and never ask. Wearing the mask of tolerance and understanding, and sating my suffering in solitude, making sure I rely on my energy alone, and never hers.

I try my best to always present an image of strength. As much as she swears to honesty and compassion, she can never accept my weakness. Why and how long can I maintain this futile facade?

And what will the outcome be?

. . . .

Hello Dad,

I'm having a lazy Sunday languishing in a sultry sea-blown sun. Actually, not lazy; I am just playing today. Running, tennis, riding to the beach, watering my plants, and lying in the sun writing to you. There is a vast difference between laziness and deliberate irresponsibility.

I lie here in new surroundings, naked in my tiny backyard, which has been landscaped for quiet and privacy. It is small, edged by a tall redwood fence and an extravagant variety of flowers. There is a small terra cotta statue of some god in the corner and an ever-changing number and variety of cats who live here. A block away is the community center, with a small park where today a string ensemble is playing

Pachelbel and Debussy, and sweet music rides the breeze to my little house.

I guess you'd call my house charming. It's a two story Victorian in the old historic section of downtown: quiet, dreamy, exclusive. It is painted in the three-tone San Francisco style. It is well furnished inside with fine antiques, an excellent stereo—everything coordinated and well done without being overdone. The woman I live with is a little spaced out, but she lets me be me and that is all I ask. Also, she's planning on moving soon; thus I can choose her replacement.

My life is still pretty borderline. Complacency is no closer to me than serenity, understanding, self-love or those other exotic countries somewhere across the ocean. Work is despair, money is still a noose around my neck, love is loneliness, friendship a fraud, knowledge a burden, and the future a vast chasm I am always on the verge of tumbling into. I live my life from fear and not love nor beauty; I find myself pathetic and repulsive much of the time. And most of my days are spent regretting the one before or fearing tomorrow.

But I am sorting through a lot, better able to distinguish bullshit from reality. There is much struggle to decide what is worth hanging onto, and what must change, but I think most of my pains are growing pains and not old wounds festering away.

Who knows, if I don't scare myself to death, perhaps someday I'll have the life and love and freedom I crave. I wonder what the cost?

I hope it's not my sensitivity. I feel a lot of pressure to be hard, to be heavy and callous, cold. I prefer the beauty, and the sadness. But that implies a profound capacity for loneliness, and this world will not tolerate loneliness, although it is driven by it.

Paul

My Dear Son,

Your description of your new home fills me with warmth and relief. You deserve such a setting, and are well-equipped—better than most anyone else I have known—to experience and appreciate all the comfort and tranquility it offers. (Pachelbel and Debussy riding the breeze to your backyard, eh? Delightful.)

With all your despair and struggle, I have to say that you have your priorities right: to try to find your way, but not at the cost of your sensitivity. I have experienced that same pressure, from so many quarters: to be hard, to be businesslike (i.e. callous). Do not give in to it; it will prove worth whatever it takes to resist that.

Compassionately,
Dad

Home from work, struggling for peace of mind against a looming tidal wave of frustration and fear.

Trauma and drama with Marie for days now. Each encounter leaves us exhausted and bruised, scared. Unable to identify the conflict, unable to let it be, we struggle on, trying to sustain our young and tender love. So fragile.

I am not a good lover these days. Preoccupied, heavy with worry, always in need of something I can't find, within or without. So lonely and hungry for love. My love.

Amazingly I survive. In its clumsy, almost way, my life continues. Graced by the beauty of Marie, of Matt, of Dad. Insulted by my job, my habits, my situation.

I feel like Kafka's cockroach, craving understanding. Marie cannot understand me, but she loves me, and challenges me to change. She inspires me with her strength, and she lacerates me with her hardness. She has made her way through life by a ruthless power which denies any weakness or hesitation.

So what is she doing with me? If I could discover what I have that she needs, I would not fear losing her. As is, my life is burdened by the terror of such a potential loss. I drive her away by the one thing she cannot tolerate: fear.

. . . .

Less and less am I able to sleep. The time weighs heavily upon me. I fill it with many things, meaning I avoid what truly must need doing.

I try to be calm and philosophical about it, but I cannot deny my feelings, resist my emotions for long. They are always waiting to jump forth and be recognized whenever my forced attention wanes. I study, I read, I have sex with myself, I contemplate adventure, I pace, I try to sleep, but only drugs work to still my—my what? Anguish comes to mind, but it is from an old poem somewhere.

Pain too, but much too much cliché. I am merely anxious. I tire of putting words to such things. Definition is a useless game. It creates distance by creating objects, when really all there is is me, pronounced by my reactions. I react, of course, tonight, to Marie—mon amie absent. We are in a forced separation. A trial, so to speak. But whose? My first reaction is childish hurt; how dare she not want to be with me? Next is fear. Is her love waning, is it lost, have I failed, am I not enough? Next is anger. Dammit, doesn't she see I love her intensely? Is she too frail or stupid to deal with that? Then comes frustration, from mis-directed anger. Of course she is neither frail nor stupid. She is much stronger than I. Then of course is confusion. What *can* be wrong? *Is* anything wrong?

And finally despair.

I love Marie. Meaning I like her, I am inspired by her. That is all that is needed. Alas though, there is one thing more. I need her. That is my failing. That is what frightens her and me. That is what fosters resentment. I risk to say that she does not need me, and that that is where her power over me lies. But I am learning never to assume, to expect or anticipate the unknown.

. . . .

Nothing changes and frustration mounts. Time blows past me like a hurricane, knocking me down and burying me in past debris.

I get nowhere. I am a man of strong impulses, yet no clear ideas. Without a true desire to exist, I can find no stability. I wander without goals. Marie is an inspiration. But she too frustrates me. She is a complex, controlled woman far beyond my comprehension, and though I respect her, I cannot understand her. I want to live my life as she does, but I can't see how. With her help, though, her example and support, I might just pull it off. It seems like such a long shot, though. I am always on the verge of failure.

. . . .

Hello my friend,

Jesus, it seems so long since I've written. Is it really September? Am I really twenty-five? Are we really growing old so fast, jumping those hurdles on the racetrack of life? Or is it death? Saul Bellow says that death is the only true god.

Hmm, this is beginning to sound rather morbid, though I don't feel that way. Awfully weary though. Pressure in my chest. The weight of the world or something.

Maybe just emotion. I've been awfully busy lately. Not much time to indulge in emotion. Feelings have been given the back seat. And back seat drivers are such a pain in the ass.

In some ways it's good though. With so much to do, there's no time to squander emotion. Ambiguity has no place in the life of a young man struggling for reality, security, stability.

Saul Bellow also says that stability can never be obtained until one is determined, committed to exist. I haven't crossed that hurdle yet, I guess. Been reading lots of existential literature lately. It's having quite an effect on me. I think I like it. But it means sacrificing my idealism for responsibility. I begin to realize that nothing is going to happen unless I create it. The question is: what do I want to have happen?

I sit here in my little garden in the dense, misty night—paper lit by flood light, table strewn with the delicate, vividly red petals of the fuchsia bushes which surround me.

What, you ask, am I so busy doing? Well, survival is a pretty full time job. Teetering here on the brink, as usual. I work three nights a week at the oyster bar. I work a few days at another restaurant doing piece-meal prep work. Five or six hours a day spent painting the house. School is looming just over the next rise. Some tennis, a little sleep; I study French. And, of course, there's Marie. Wow, is there ever Marie.

What a challenge. I've certainly got a tiger by the tail, with this complex, dynamic, profoundly intelligent, beautiful, always-changing woman who has beguiled and enraptured me. Love is the greatest adventure for me. And I have struck gold. Marie is prodding me, seducing me, tricking me, frustrating me, daring me to grow up, to awaken, to blossom, to finally acknowledge myself. I think, just maybe, with a lot of luck, some good timing, an awesome amount of work, pain, and of course beauty, things are going to work out very well for our hero here: this person that is me.

Keep your fingers crossed.

I love you,
Paul

Hi—

A year ago you had just left and I was trying to put my feelings about that leaving into words. We've only been together once since then—physically, that is. Some good peaceful times here lately. Fall is distinctly in the air; I have been busy with a lot of projects, such as much fence repair with a neighbor, but with some good relaxing times alone, too.

I think that our being away in Wyoming recently, plus having people like Les and Allison here helps to clear my vision as to what I have in my life and this place. Obviously my movements and my contacts are extremely limited here—almost restricted to just a wife—for long periods, and I have to be careful to keep my balance, to keep my perceptions accurate.

Had some lovely times with Leslie and Allison; they like coming here. And getting acquainted with such a brand new person is an impressive experience for me, one not easy to get into the right words, perhaps. I think she has very good parents.

The photos of the jewelry box you made for Marie are exquisite—I'm eager to see it in person. The book which I sent you recently is the birthday gift I had so much trouble finding. Before Christmas I saw a teleplay on educational TV "Christmas Snows, Christmas Winds" and proceeded to write around to obtain a copy of the script, because it was so moving for me. This eventually led me to the book containing it and several other short stories from the library, and to write the author in Provo. He was in London on sabbatical, but after several months and several phone calls, I reached him back home in Utah and had a most rewarding conversation. His suggestions finally allowed me to find copies of his book—so here it is. You may want to start by reading "Christmas Snows." Some very sensitive writing.

Love,
Dad

Hello Dad,

It's late; I sit in my room trying to unwind from work. Though it's very warm and the air is motionless, it still feels very refreshing after the evening spent before the ovens of the little bakery where I work now.

Nothing much new to report. Lots of heaviness, self-pity, fear. Haven't much to say, but I'm feeling very alone, so I must communicate somehow. Incredible stress from school, so much work and worry and resistance. For what? Not knowing where it leads, it's still all that I have to go on at this point. So very little. My heart isn't in it. But where is it? Where have I lost it?

This feeling overwhelms me. The fear paralyzes me. My reactions only serve to perpetuate the cycle. Immediately my self-image and confidence drop. I am nothing. I am a stupid ugly little boy dwarfed in a world of antagonistic giants, powerful, sure, and ruthless. Communication stops. I become humble and meek, uninteresting—and people react accordingly: ignoring me. And I react accordingly: hating myself and craving release.

Just when I need to be the strongest (when the going gets tough . . .) I fall apart. It feels like a no-win situation.

Marie only frustrates this. She is powerful, assured; she knows what she wants and who she is and she doesn't falter. When things get tough, she just compensates, and becomes focused on the problem until it is resolved. She is a complex, controlled woman far beyond the comprehension of this man-boy, who has so foolishly opened himself up wide to the winds of her power. She is my home, my reason to be, because I have no past to build on. But I should know better than to base my life on another's, and when I remember that, I am so alone, because I haven't myself to fall back on.

If you see myself wandering around Colorado, please send him out; I need him badly.

Must close,
Paul

Dear Paul,

A typical hunting-season day: grey and heavy overhead, muddy underfoot, cozy indoors. A time to feel and relish the warmth of this house. A time to contemplate.

Got your pensive and pained letter. I hear you clearly— don't have any wisdom to respond with. I puzzle a good deal, and wonder if you do, over my inconsistency. Feeling so good at times (not always with identifiable reasons)—so awful at others (not always with identifiable reasons). Wish it was always as good as at the best times. (I think I do, anyway.)

But I've changed my opinion about consistency in people somewhat. It seems too often the hallmark of those who impose invented "feelings" in order to keep subsurface what really goes on inside: the even-tempered ones, the positive thinkers, etc. If my life isn't uniformly happy, then it's dishonest to try to pretend it is. So I laugh some, and cry some—and very often wonder why.

I'm sending some good photos of the completed cradle; see how you like it. I'm really eager for Christmas time and a chance to see you again—and Marie.

Love,
Dad

Dear Dad,

The first rains of winter seductively present themselves. Though feeble and unsure, their bluff works, and the streets of Santa Cruz are unusually quiet as people cower inside their little clapboard forts, unsure of how to deal with this heavy humid gloom.

I know better, though, than to be chased inside, alone, where silence and emptiness lurk in the shadows and one is at the mercy of one's emotion. No, my heart is bound and bruised enough by the fears and tribulations of everyday life; no need to deliberately expose it to the brutal power of primordial sorrow. Thus, I try to stay outdoors as much as possible, or at least I switch locations often, to keep distraction on duty.

No major changes to report. Same house, same job, same lover and daily routines. Seem to be holding my own in this silly world. Barely, it seems, but compared to what? School: I study French, something I find very therapeutic in that it keeps me in the moment—

114

it keeps my mind from running its endless laps around my muddy mundane track. I can't get enough French. It fascinates me. A class in energy, resources and environmental design. Also fascinating, a little frightening, and very practical. Readings by Commoner, etc. Projects include designs for retrofitting our houses. My quarter project is an energy-design evaluation of the bakery; they're getting ready to do a remodel, so I hope to come up with some ways to save some energy, space, and money. Very interesting project. Also an independent study in residential architecture. Studying the theories of Wright, Corbusier, Greene and Greene. Finally, a class in African Dance. Incredible form of release; dancing and singing with a large group of people. In the absence of money for therapy, African dance does very well.

Not much happening socially. A movie here or there, glancing at Time magazine while sitting on the john, etc. Finding it easier and easier to make new friends though. In this world of fear and uncertainty, folks are starting to band together, to open up, to communicate.

Marie is as incredible as ever. Probably the most complex person I've ever gotten close to. She, too, is overwhelmed by all this confusion and responsibility, but she seems much more graceful in her reactions to it. I'm learning lots from her.

Paul

. . . .

Why is it I fear being well? Do I really crave death, or do I merely fear life? There's no dignity, no passion, in fearing life. Everyone is afraid. But to crave death? Is this some confused message crying out from my genes: give up, give up; it doesn't matter, nothing matters, why suffer?

What would happen if I chose to live? Have I got what I need? First I must be sure I am totally purged of my wish for death: my out, my excuse for never trying.

If I was committed to living, if I refused to acknowledge the possibility, the potential for escape from pain by death; if I could eliminate that choice, I might have myself—and a life worth living.

If

If

115

If

If I can find the key to my need to suffer, maybe I can find something to live for.

. . . .

The unexplainable sorrows grow heavier, and expand out into the world. I am unable to shake them off, as I shuffle through day after empty, silent day.

Death seems inevitable. My momentum into darkness is beyond my control.

Paul and I talked on the phone frequently during this period. He was, I think, quite candid with me, and I grew increasingly alarmed about him. I groped and struggled for a resolution. I found none. At one grim point I wrote in my journal:

What does Paul feel? Think? Numbly, mostly. Not clearly. In considerable confusion. He doesn't seem angry, usually, nor sad. He is scared—desperate. He feels distaste for his self, for his past. He is terribly worried, dreading, defeated about his future.

He used to think it would be, while perhaps somewhat difficult, a generally benevolent world; he has not found it so. He feels he has tried extremely hard, worked extremely hard, and accomplished nothing. He has not found his way—his career—his life. He has not prepared himself for living in this world. Others have. He sees them all about him. Passing him by.

Sometimes, he sees the world as unreal, sick—and his pain as an accurate response to that world. But not consistently. Often, he seems to yearn for a career direction, for success, for accomplishment, for inspiration. Such confusion!

Altogether (and he senses this) he is no different than he was last year, the year before, seven years ago—deep inside. I'm afraid that he may be in enough despair that he could blow his job, his education, his relationships—his existence!

I cannot see a solution. I am no help, except a distant ear to listen. He has no one.

Thanksgiving Day. A lesson in aloneness. But is it acknowledged, or self imposed? Why can't people work together? Why does it seem so ludicrous to ask someone who loves you for support? So hard to be yourself when the expression of that self is reflected back as such ugliness. I love Marie, and I feel that that entitles me to just show and share exactly how I feel. But no, it certainly doesn't seem to work like that. I'm more alone than ever. Love seems to be such a tease, taunting me with possible fulfillment, union. Marie seems so right, and I so ridiculously wrong. Always making a fool of myself trying to follow my inclinations.

Floating around in this huge void, searching for something real, and poor Marie seems the only stable thing I can grasp onto, and I end up strangling her. My God, she's so beautiful. And I'm suffocating that beauty in my desperation for love.

I'm not an evil man, I'm just sensitive beyond my means to comprehend. Feelings too powerful to incorporate. A sensitivity that could be so powerful if it were in my control, but in my clumsy hands, I destroy everything I touch.

She is she, and I am . . . ? Lost. Driven by a passion that is violent in its need for resolution, for expression. Answers seem so far away. My imagination leads me on, but my gut is endlessly falling into a bottomless chasm of raging, empty pain.

Give it time, Paul. Keep trying. Don't give up, yet. Believe in yourself, even if you cannot define your struggle. Try to believe in yourself. Just a little longer.

Paul finally made it through this most tortured time, and he and Marie did come to Colorado to visit us in the woods during the holidays. It was good for all of us; we talked, we hiked, we feasted, I played music for them—and they returned to Santa Cruz.

Dad,

Today is the day before school starts, the last few moments of quiet. Time speeds up and anxiety rises with the sun.

It's raining profusely, the sky sweats out its toxic build-ups. For days now, the wind has blown ferociously, oscillating between burning fever and aching chill. The air became electric, a house twelve miles away disintegrated in a lightning bolt, and the explosion woke me, shaken with immediate fear of earthquake or atomic war. Now the streets are full of water, twelve to eighteen inches deep, creeping up doorsteps, filling cellars, and low-riding sports cars.

I never like being inside when I have a choice. Stupidly, instead of staying home and being productive and effective, I bundle up in acres of raingear and trudge clumsily through the storm.

Santa Cruz doesn't feel too good. That elusive vacation clarity of mind soon dissipates when confronted by the granite reality of everyday life and the struggle for existence.

Still, I gained much strength and inspiration from my time in Colorado. Life seems more of a game than a war. Unfortunately, I got a kit without rules included, and I think a couple of the pieces may be missing too.

Shit, my mind is aimlessly wandering. Alien thoughts creep out from hiding in the dark dusty recesses, spies sent out to sabotage my calm.

All I really wanted to say was:

Dad, it was *good* to be with you again.

Love,
Paul

Dear Paul,

Yes it was good to be together again. A fine setting in which to experience each other. I'll never forget this time. You looked well, but showed the signs of recent strains, too. Life registers the effects of our struggles on our bodies, unfailingly. If you come to Colorado after graduation, perhaps you can spend some time here. And if I get a chance, I'll try to come to Santa Cruz again, too. Keep me posted on your plans for Primal Therapy.

I guess I think of you every day—and I love you.

Dad

Dad,

Noontime at Neary's Lagoon, a small area near my old house

that sits in the lowlands; filled with water, cattails, willows, duckweed, and lots and lots of birds. A long wooden pathway/bridge winds through the lagoon, with benches and gazebos for lovers, grandparents, solitary wanderers, and others. I come here often with stale bread from the bakery for the birds. Sometimes I study here; sometimes Marie comes and we drink wine and spend rich precious time alone with each other. There are always children to watch, or swans, reflections, clouds—anything but my own thoughts and feelings.

It is only the third day of classes, yet already I am overcome with anxiety. Fear kept me from class today, and I hide here with the ducks and the preschoolers, seemingly more my level these days.

This will be a rough quarter. Because of time lost during the flood, we have school Saturdays and holidays. Much time was lost too, from work, and the politicians have cut most of my financial aid. I am tired of being poor. My life feels like suffering, punishment, or sometimes just the avoidance of such.

I wonder why this strong, oh-so-strong, reaction to school?

I wonder why I persist with such sickness?

I wonder where to find the strength to either quit or change?

Also I wonder how my life seems to hold itself together in spite of all this. I anxiously await the time when I am in control of it, and not at the mercy of it. Do you think this is possible? Well, somehow that change is already occurring. Somehow things seem more OK. From somewhere there is strength.

Marie sends her regards; she was really taken with you.

Thanks for your letter.

Paul

. . . .

Marie and I must separate. Why?

Because we can't be together. So simple. She says for just a while, but a day feels like a year. What will a month feel like, or a year; or will it be a lifetime? How to keep from going numb?

And why does she hang on to me so? Why not just let me go, set me adrift? What is freedom, and what is emptiness? And why can't two people in love be together?

And why can't one person in love be alone?

Hi-

Had a period of some clarity last night, I think, following your painful phone call concerning Marie. I'd like to tell you how your recent trauma looks from here—hoping that a distant view (by an observer whom you know well) will prove helpful.

You had a bit of special insight about the problems of someone very close to you, and felt inclined to offer help. Her particular pain prevented her from receiving your inputs straight, and, as it always does, her old shit and yours interacted—with resulting fireworks. She probably said some things which were accurate—and many which were not. No, you didn't deserve what you suffered. But we seldom do. Justice hardly happens, I'm afraid.

This episode needn't be accepted as an authentic reflection of your own neurosis. I don't have a trustworthy impression of Marie's strengths and weaknesses. But her own pain undoubtedly beclouds her perception of your real insides. It cannot be otherwise, for any of us. In the midst of such pain levels by two people trying to relate to each other, valid impressions of oneself are most elusive—nearly impossible.

I thought anew about what Paul is really like: bright, sensitive, compassionate, creative, both clever and wise and in considerable pain and confusion at this point, in my view. One of the finest people I've ever known.

I hope you're taking good care of him.

Love,
Dad

Sleepless, drunk, agitated beyond belief.

I cannot sever myself from Marie. And sever is how it feels. I know what I want, and I cannot have it. And it tears me apart, because I remember how it was in the womb, when there was no separation between need and fulfillment.

Now it is all need, pounding on me, tearing at me, thrashing me about. And relief is just an idea that exists because pain must have an opposite.

Round and round we go.

Primal Therapy is a form of psychotherapy which was first introduced in the late sixties in California. It is intended for helping individuals work their way out of troublesome personal symptoms and behavior (neurosis, if you will) and into the securing of peace, of self-fulfillment, of resolution. It is a quite intense, demanding, long term approach based upon the concept that, in many people, much life-long distress, discomfort, ill-health, trouble in relationships, feelings of non-fulfillment, etc., can be traced to very early painful experiences: those happening to us in the first years, months, days, even minutes after birth—and, in many cases, during the months preceding birth. Further, that in these early, unformed stages, the infant person is inexperienced to pain of all kinds— physical and psychological—and reacts instinctively to suppress even "low levels" of pain, which he does not perceive as low levels at all. That the universal reaction to such pain is to shut down the neurological circuits within the body which transmit such feelings of pain to the consciousness, and thereby reduce the hurt. But at a tragic price, because forever after (failing some extremely powerful method of healing), the feeling "circuits" will continue to be damaged and dysfunctional, rendering the individual insensitive to some, or many, feelings of pain—and also to feelings of pleasure—the same set of circuits being needed to transmit both kinds: pain and pleasure.

The originators of Primal Therapy reasoned that because these early painful feelings had been instinctively blocked or repressed (with a lifetime of tragic symptoms resulting), that resolution and cure might come if the ancient feelings could be truly experienced—felt in their full intensity and put to rest once and for all. By reliving enough of the truly pivotal fearsome experiences (more accurately by actually fully living them for the very first time), and integrating that knowing deep inside, one would finally know peace, health and rightness—even if forty years later.

I had extensive first-hand familiarity with the technique over a period of many years by this time in Paul's life, and had experienced dramatically helpful effects on myself and in my life as a result; I trusted it.

It had been my perception, over a long period of time, that most other approaches of psychotherapy and psychiatry seemed to achieve positive results all too rarely. But, I had seen that many persons had benefited from this technique, so I was eager to see Paul committed to it. He was familiar with it; he had watched my transformation over nearly ten years; he was at a nearly desperate point in his own life.

And so, even though it meant a traumatic disruption in his life (he was within barely three months of completing the requirements for a degree in architecture), he made the decision to leave Santa Cruz and move to Denver, where there were practitioners whom I knew well and trusted, to commit himself to a very serious involvement with Primal Therapy.

This choice was to color his life, almost daily, for the next several years. Not that this pivotal decision came instantly—nor easily. It did not.

The time draws near for a major change, perhaps the greatest I've made or will make. That's what I'm hoping for anyway. So let's chronicle this strange journey. So, where are we starting this search from; for what and why? Big questions, huh?

Well, you see, there's this mountain of pain in front of me, and giant boulders keep rolling off and trying to smash me. And I can't seem to dodge them fast enough; I can't run fast enough, and every once in a while one crashes into me, or almost, and I'm all cut up and bruised. What's worse, I'm just scared to death of getting smashed, and so I keep frantically dashing around dodging boulders of pain, even when none are falling. It's really starting to wear me out.

The earth begins to rumble and my foundations start to shake. Time to tear up my dried and fragile roots and take flight, like a seed.

· · · · · · ·

Through Primal Therapy I hope to resolve and to integrate my past, a past I have failed to recognize. By coming to terms with this history, sorting out what is really me and what is not me, I hope to finally be able to acknowledge the reality of the present, and to realize the future. I want to be moving toward something, not running away. I want to change the motivation of my life from fear to joy. I want to explore, not to hide. I want to change my view of life from one of struggle, to one of adventure. I want some peace of mind.

· · · · · · ·

Playing strange games, serious for sure, but distasteful. Playing with death, making sure I have an easy out, should I find the strength and the clarity of mind. A little box in the back of a drawer, labeled "quick and clean", like a spy with his cyanide pill.

But that little box of death causes me great discomfort. Its powerful forces both attract and repel me intensely. It forces me to make a commitment. He lives, he lives not, he lives, he lives not, he . ·. .

How does one understand such a thing? This must truly be one of the great human questions: why tolerate lives of sadness and suffering, awkwardness and abuse?

My great fear is caused by lack of faith, both of the within and the without. Is this lack caused by ignorance, and absence of any positive experience which might affirm my potential? Or is it caused by wisdom? There has been a richness to my life which implies the possibility for graceful and profound being. Yet there is also the negative side: the evil, dishonest and cowardly nature of Paul. Which is the more real? And what of the pain, which is oh-so-real, and comes sweeping out of the sky like a harsh, screaming bird of prey, lusting for my spirit?

Ahh, I see too much. Yet I understand so little. So very, very little.

· · · · · · ·

Dad,

It's been a while. God, life is so intense right how; not overtly, or definably, but I can feel the push and pull of so many forces upon me, from both within and without.

An old friend from Durango just left after a few days. His companionship was invaluable at this time. He is a very straightforward, articulate, and sensitive man, and time spent with him is always very reassuring. He has spent a few years in Primal Therapy, and had some valuable insights to add, to aid me in coming to grips with the next few months.

Leaving Santa Cruz is going to be (actually is) a wrenching experience. It feels so much like home here: the town, countryside, people, my goals and ideas, Marie. And sacrificing that to move to a disgusting place like Denver. For what? What am I doing; what is going to become of me? Why must I keep running?

I'm so scared, Dad. To be all alone again, in a strange place, without a home, without money of my own, and confronted by the task of feeling all the pain and anguish of twenty-five years—trying to pick my way through the labyrinth of defenses and fears and ugliness, with all its horrors and monsters—in search of what? Me? What if there's nothing there? So what if I eliminate neurosis and fears unrecognized; maybe that's all that I am. What happens if there's nothing else there? Is anything ever going to feel right?

Love,
Paul

Dear Paul,

Your apprehension at this point is not unanticipated—but no less painful or scary because of that, I know.

In my view, you have chosen a path requiring more insight, and more guts, than ninety-nine percent of us ever evidence. You won't be sorry you did. Once you have settled into therapy, and survived whatever disappointments and adjustments the first few days may involve, I'm confident that you will then begin to find relief and clarity. And, as I mentioned on the phone, you will actually welcome the chance to face and experience your pain squarely—with the healing which that can bring.

I hope that these strange phrases can hold enough meaning for you now, to help you carry on through a few more days until you will develop your own meanings and truths—far superior to what my poor words can hint at.

As I have observed, when we get to this point, and agonize "why the hell should I have to put myself through this?" or "what if it doesn't work?" or any of a hundred different awful feelings, it's likely that we are actually being tortured by other, more remote feelings/fears—frights remaining from other times and places, and not presently recognizable for what they really are.

I urge you to hold on—to trust me in my opinion of what the therapy can mean to you. You are right for it; it is right for you. And I feel very secure about your placing yourself in Vince's safe, comforting, and experienced hands.

I love you, and I want peace for you—almost more than I've ever wanted anything.

Dad

Up on campus cleaning up loose ends. Is this the last I'll see of it? Its beauty, and all the associations I have, the potential for a rich and real life, a place in the world that is mine—and meaningful. The guilt and regret of my past, its ugliness and waste, the same feelings and thoughts that Marie brings up—these things are tearing me apart. I have so far to go, with so much fear standing in my way.

Death becomes more and more feasible, as peace of mind becomes more and more elusive. I spent the night with Marie last night. Ah, Marie, beautiful Marie. It was so intensely beautiful to touch her once again. Our love-making was clumsy, real. Our fear of each other so apparent, as we open ourselves up wide.

I would live and die for this woman, this incredible woman. Can she ever understand the depth of my feeling for her? Is it fair to ask her to accept that responsibility? Her own reality is so raw; how can I ask her to assume mine?

. . . .

Where is the poetry?
Where is the passion?
Where is Paul?
Paul has hidden himself away, but now he's run out of places to run, he's backed into a corner with nowhere left to hide. It's the final showdown. The ultimate fight, or the ultimate flight. Which will it be?

Both are giant leaps into the unknown, staking my entire stack with no guarantee of a fair deal.

Well, the greater the risk, the greater the reward.

. . . .

Befogged, disoriented, neither alive nor dead. In shock.

How can I say these next words? I tried to end my life last night.

Late in the night by the sea at Woodrow Beach, it seemed right. I found the strength. I had to try; I had to test myself. Numbing myself with barbiturates and champagne (a good-bye gift from Judy), I thought perhaps the sea might take me. But no; even in my weakest, most unconnected, uncontrolled moments, my goddamn fucking will to live held on. My body rejected the drugs. Falling, stumbling, crawling, vomiting, I fall off the rocks into the sea. The waves knocking me up against the cliffs, bruising and slicing my flesh.

Covered with blood and vomit, soaked through layers and layers of clothing, I spend hours trying to crawl up a vertical, moss-covered cliff. Falling to the stones below, climbing and falling, bleeding and vomiting and crying, I reach the top. Unable to unlock my bike, I stagger the long miles home, weaving and tripping and running into things.

Now I sit here numb and toxic, and wonder why. Why can't I live, and why can't I die?

I tried to reach out to Marie. I went to her house, saying I needed someone to talk to. But no, she was stone, and looked at frail Paul with disgust. She stuck her hand in that giant wound which is me and she squeezed my heart hard. And it hurts my heart—actually aches—with each breath.

And yet, still I love her intensely. How cruel life is; Marie is. If she could only reach out and touch me, hold me, be with me when I hurt, then I might have the strength to carry on.

. . . .

On the verandah of Joze Cafe, sitting beneath the palms on a deliciously warm spring day.

The associations I have with Joze' are immense. Funny how I

determine the phases of my life in terms of the relationship at the time: that was when I was with Jenny, or Cindy, or Marie: not, that was when I was in Durango, or working at Falcon, etc.

Marie is champing at the bit to be free, and it is painful to watch. How can I blame her, though, and what else can I do but accept the inevitable, and try to make it all right somehow.

Sometimes I think that all Marie wants is to be accepted; perhaps that's all that any of us really wants.

. . . .

Redundancy; I'm confused and anxious to understand, reconnect, clear out and lighten up.

So hard to look into the future; my mind shuns it. Much easier to reflect upon the past—some of it anyway. Can clarity of mind and light-heartedness go hand-in-hand?

. . . .

Tomorrow I leave my home, and with no home inside, I set myself adrift in the world. As usual, things appear *almost* as if the situation for rightness is presenting itself, and perhaps there is a slight glimmer of recognition on my part, but I am unable to reach out to it, to take it in my arms.

It still feels wrong to leave Santa Cruz, but it also seems inevitable; inevitable wrongness seems the pattern of my life. I can't help feeling that I'm running again, or that I've been forced out, or that I'm missing out, losing ground, avoiding the truth—living fantasies and illusions, unable to face the reality of my situation.

Yet I can't let myself resist it; I must dive in with the little faith that I have in myself and the world. And the world has really been very wonderful to me—everyone but Marie, from whom I expect so much, and who is incapable (or just lacks the desire) of giving at all.

I long for the time when I can view our encounter in life with clarity, and I hope that my sensitivities prove right, and that she is the woman for me. But more, I hope that we both realize that I am the man for her. Why does that seem so much to ask?

. . . .

Grey morning; it rained all night. The air is heavy and damp. My old friend, the mourning dove, is singing (or crying, I don't know which).

I feel no strength inside, just sorrow; and beyond?

Soon to board my plane for Denver. Oh, I am wrenched apart. I have done well in this town.

And I have also caused great harm.

. . . .

At Leslie's house now, in Boulder. Spent the day walking, talking, drugging myself with coffee and alcohol. My brain was very turned on, but my heart subdued. I thought and I talked, articulate and direct—numb and repressed, anxious. Santa Cruz seemed far away, and I kept any thoughts of it at bay. I had a strong compulsion to eat, drink, smoke. I wrote a letter to Marie, and felt guilty for it.

I had lunch with Mom, and it seemed fairly clear. There has been some acceptance there. Sure hasn't been much contact with her for a while, but maybe it'll get better now.

I was afraid that I was getting my defenses up for Monday, the beginning of my Primal Therapy, because I was so cold and hard after months of irrepressible emotions in Santa Cruz. But as I lay here tonight, reminded of Marie by many things, I see that anxiety and pain are close by. I am scared by some glimmers of realizations. Not knowing if they are real or not is even more frightening.

I fear that Primal Therapy will take too long, that I will be stuck in Denver for years, never able to return to Santa Cruz as my attachments fade. I fear the loss of Marie, and with my potential for future clarity of heart, incredible sorrow.

I fear also that Primal will obliterate my defenses, and I will be unable to involve myself in the world. It makes me think that instead of opening myself up, I should be practicing at hardening myself, so I won't have to live outside of the world.

I hope I'm special; I hope this does not take too long; I hope I can overcome my fear with strength and determination, and move through this like a trout in the sun.

My ideal plans, just for the sake of future retrospection: to blow, flow, dance my way through Primal here, till I get a handle on it and feel like I can carry it with me anywhere. Then:
- to finish school
- to study French
- to clear and build my body
- to find good, strong work, and save up enough money for a return to Santa Cruz and school, with a car, some confidence, peace of mind, and myself—my *self*—*my* self.

· · · · · · ·

Well, the battle begins. Unable to sleep, I will continue to converse with me. I guess, true to the process, I won't try to direct my thoughts, but let them come as they will, order or no.

There are so many people backing me in this, backing me even without any knowledge of what I'm doing, believing in me and their responses to me. How much, so much, strength this gives me. I cannot very well believe in myself by myself; I need others' support (or approval?).

Can I define my problems, the manifestations of them?
- Primarily, an inability to trust myself, believe in myself and my ability to cope with life. Fear of failure.
- An ineptness at clearly comprehending situations beyond their reactive symbolism.
- A need to dull, deaden myself (or stimulate myself sometimes).
- A terrible anxiousness when things are unresolved.
- An inability to apply myself fully.
- Lack of clear memory.
- Envy of others' capabilities, and subsequent feelings of my own helplessness, inadequacy.
- Distorted body image.
- Vomiting and distress with food.
- An overabundant need to give—maybe.
- Guilt, lots. Feelings of letting people down.
- Jealousy and possessiveness.

- Inclination to give in, to give up (or die).
- Self-hate.

How to best facilitate the process:
- No drugs.
- Lots of quiet.
- Little distraction, worries of future finances, regret of past, thinking of people far away.
- Reducing intellectualization, putting words or images to feelings—except when useful associations might help set me off.
- Not putting time limitations or expectations on it.
- Trying to believe in my self—I think that I do somehow, or I wouldn't be here.
- Not giving in to sleep.

To give up so much to do this is a brave and risky thing, I'm beginning to think.

In many ways Paul was an ideal candidate for this therapy. He definitely had enough troublesome symptoms to convince him that he needed something; he had felt these long enough to be in dead earnest about going for it; he had eight or ten years of close experience in observing its effects on me; he had read possibly everything published to that date relating to it; and he had already had helpful discussions with skilled workers in that therapy.

Then the day came—the day to begin to experience, first hand, the things he had anticipated, feared, contemplated from more angles than I can possibly imagine. He was not quite twenty-six.

Primal Times
The Twenty-seventh Year

Morning. A windy day, chilly yet sunny. I sit on the south deck. Up early, I try to prepare myself for the coming day, my first in Primal Therapy. Tears come to my eyes.

I read Janov, I reflect on Marie (instant anxiety), I try to sit quietly and feel the wind on my skin, the beating of my heart, the tightness in my gut. A journey of ten thousand miles begins with a single step.

I think a bit of Leslie. It has been sometimes hard to be with her, to view her struggle, her need, her vagueness. To see her living in a difficult situation in a home with an angry man. I think of Mom, but not too carefully; I don't want her too clearly defined, for I feel I will have to soon tear her apart in my mind. I think of Dad, so sensitive yet so strong, guiding me along on this bizarre and frightening journey.

. . . .

I sit here in the park now, smoking. Reading over these notes, I suddenly begin to hyperventilate, breathing rapidly and choppily. I can hardly wait to get to the Primal Center and lie on the floor. My body is trembling. Tears flow freely.

Yes, I can do this, I am ready. I am desperate to do this. I am frantic for freedom. I feel the wind blowing past me, through me, and I am ready to blow apart.

Yes, he was ready; he was motivated; he was equipped. And he waded in with all the fullness of his soul.
Then he returned from his first session:

Afternoon. Three hours with Vince—I dropped into my body feelings right away. Head back, body rolled up, gagging and choking. Pains in my gut reminded me of time spent in the hospital at age ten or so, to have my tonsils out. Pains in my back reminded me of falling off my bike at age seven.

Took a ride past the old house on Kearney, Mount Airy Hospital, Irene's house, etc. Hard to stay long. Went for a run, sat in the hot tub drinking wine and smoking. Scared—I'm obviously backed against the wall.

Talking with Vince afterward, the situation is so awesome. My early life appears to be nothing *but* pain. My pattern has been flight, to close down. Now I must learn to fight. I am so overwhelmed by my task, and my situation. Totally at the mercy of so many things. And there is definitely a mountain of pain to confront.

And I am still running, afraid to commit myself. But also, the prospect intrigues me. The ideas excite me. To really understand the total formation of my personality and all its manifestations, relationships, perspectives, motivations. It slowly begins to take on the appearance of a grand, and very bizarre, adventure.

How to dive in, how to dedicate myself? It's unfortunate that my past has taught me to hide, to run. If I was a fighter like Marie, I would power through this like a steamroller. Perhaps I can use her inspiration, her example. Also, Marie taught me how to surrender myself. I must surrender myself to Vince, to Primal, to my *self.*

I am not alone.

My *body* is my access; it remembers. Not my *mind.* I must keep it as clear as possible.

Are you strong?

Yes!

Are you determined?

Yes!

Are you scared?

Jesus fucking Christ *yes* I'm scared!!!

. . . .

Washington Park on a glorious spring day. My body is aching, my throat raw from screaming in Primal sessions, my gut tortured by remembered pain. Each day I carry it a little farther—I cry harder and deeper, I go back more and more.

I have yet to truly go back to *that* place though, and be there, though I crave it so much. Still, more and more falls into place; the connections and insights astound me.

Vince said a very kind thing today. Without my saying anything to him, he realized how much I want to clear this and return to California. He said that he knows I don't want to stay in Denver, for even a year, and he will do his best to optimize the process, sharing secrets with me that will help.

My access is through two ways: primarily, my body, of course; but when it becomes afraid, my words help to remind me. Talking about situations which will trigger my body to respond. How good it feels to surrender to this—and to know that inside, beyond all the pain and defenses, is *me*. Someone whose appearance I anxiously await, and who, in his way, anxiously awaits expression, and a chance to live free. Vince is very similar to me, and it helps him know how to move with his empathy.

The scary thing is, I think you've got to take the process all the way. Once you get started, there's no turning back, and if you get stuck halfway, it could be very ugly.

. . . .

Hello Dad,

Well, I'm about three days into it, now. Needing to connect, I'm not sure why. You'd think by now I'd be tired of writing. Writing and feeling (at least trying to); that's been life these past few days.

I guess mostly I want to say thanks for all that you've done to help me reach this place. It's a strange, awesome journey I've begun, a rocky road full of peril and undeniable pain. But I recognize it as the only way home. And I've got on my running shoes; with a little luck, I may just sprint the whole way. Wouldn't that be nice! Vince is working out exceptionally well. We have a lot in common (pain that is), and I think it creates a strong empathy which gives him some rich insight into how to proceed.

So far it feels like some very intriguing adventure. I'm just fascinated by the process, and delighted by the wealth, clarity, and ease of insights. Somehow I fear, though, as I surrender to it more and more, that I may be in for a harsh and brutal encounter. I don't know yet; it would be nice if I could just save the pain for therapy time, and carry on a somewhat light-hearted life outside of those quiet, dark rooms. Light-heartedness may not be feasible in Denver. But it's one of my goals in therapy, and because it came up, I know that it's in there somewhere. It's an amazing feeling to trust myself.

Somehow I think this is going to work, to really work. That hope, and that profound anticipation of relief, are so delicious. There's a lot to talk about. I hope to see you soon.

Thanks, Dad,
Paul

I had, of course, been waiting anxiously to begin hearing of Paul's reaction to his therapy, and I was gratified to know that he felt good about his beginning. I purposely continued to avoid calling or writing him for a while longer, believing that it was best not to interject any of myself, a parent, at such a crucial time in his inner explorations. And, I was worried that, as sometimes happens, his delving into the past would leave him unable to continue a close and loving relationship with me. Fortunately, that did not happen in his case.

High anxiety, unable to sleep. My body is tense, aching, it wants to let something out. But Leslie's house is not the place. So I'll try to write it out.

I realize, as I lie here thinking of my situation: no home, car, money etc., that my anxiety is one of helplessness. Once again, I put myself at the mercy of the world, and it scared me the first time, and it scares me now. Oh man, does it scare me! My heart starts pounding, it's hard to breathe, my body itches all over.

Also, reading a letter from Marie, she talks of seeking unattachment, aloneness, and this brings something up in me: rejection? I know I had put a lot of my trust in the world on Marie. It was she that carried me along, and when she writes of cutting off that support! Whew! Ouch! Aarrgghh!

. . . .

Back home after a weekend in Boulder with Les. The weekend wasn't too good; it's too easy to be compulsive at Leslie's house, smoking, drinking, eating. Maybe there are just too many reminders there, but I find too many distractions, too.

I want to fast for a few days and see if it helps. I say that as I sit here smoking and drinking black tea. Where is my will? And is it right to exercise it now? Well, fasting should clear my body out; it's a bit numb at this point, and I need it to be clear again.

The session was hard. This weekend, with its too-many, too-varied contacts, plus looking at lots of pictures from the past; it just brought up too much. I overloaded, and went into the session like a rock. My resistance to Vince was intense. He really had to push, and eventually the sadness and hurt came out. Sadness at being so stifled, ignored, suffocated.

Went out with Mom and talked pretty frankly. She's scared, but she's behind me too. I think she's really learning from all this.

I still can't get Marie off my mind. So much hurt and resentment, I want to just say good-bye, to tell her to leave me alone, because I can't seem to adjust myself to accepting the little bit she cares to give, and it seems easier to deal with the pain of loss rather than the agonizing uncertainty of what is happening now. But I can't seem to let go of her. I want her deeply involved in my life, and I in hers, and she's just not ready. She's too young, or I'm not right, or perhaps she just has no need for that close a relationship.

Godammit it hurts to love so hard and not have it be right, not have it be accepted or reciprocated. It really tests my belief in myself.

·······

Grey sunset, sitting on a concrete bench in the littlest patch of nature here in the city, but it's all I could find. There are birds, and a tiny bit of grass, a slimy little creek full of trash and metropolitan pathogens. Ohhh, I ache. It's not pain, and it's not freedom. I'm stuck in that bleak, dreary in-between. I hate this feeling, this dullness, drab heartache. This no-man's land of indefinable suffering. Out of the corner of my mind I begin to see my reality, the harshness of my situation here. It's more than some have, but it's not enough for me. There's so much more available, to me.

Talked in session with Vince about women today. With Marie so sharply on my mind, I thought I could clear some stuff up. And my brain *could* see the connections, the patterns, relating to my mother, my needs for touch, for acceptance, for help in accepting myself. I *knew* all of this; but I can't seem to get down into it and clear it. There must be some terrible hurt inside, cause I'm sure scared to confront it.

Searching for ways to trigger myself: movies, music, photos, thoughts, places and people.

Godammit I'm stuck.

Godammit I want to get unstuck.

Godammit I didn't ask for this burden, these stones I carry around inside of me.

The old, deep realities that come to a person while reliving early painful experiences in therapy often are not easily communicated in words by the person experiencing them. Many are pre-verbal; many are not felt as cerebral, but as deep physical sensations—reflecting all those truths somehow recorded in the circuits and tissues of our bodies. And the achieving of relief, of clarity, of peace often discovered at the end of a good session usually causes the participant to feel that it is too important and too personal to even bother to try to talk about. It feels more crucial to integrate the truths internally than to try to explain them to anyone else.

A solemn day, grey and cold. Feeling sad. Sensing a loss or a subtle flavor of tragedy about myself. My life seems so clumsy, always on the verge of falling apart. What was the quote? "A man of high ideas and aspirations, unable to motivate himself, to affect his imagination."

I feel young and immature today; my human contacts are awkward. I am disappointed. I can't stop thinking of the people around me, and throughout my life, whose lives seem so graceful and easy. Some of them clear, some just very well defined in a kind of beautiful, easy way, that makes the formation of their personality—even if built around pain—seem right.

I am filled with regret about the wasteful way I've run my life. I begin to comprehend what an awesome task it is to change oneself. It feels almost out of reach. I can see how it might be possible, but I don't feel the strength inside of me. I feel like just drying up and blowing away with the breeze. That's kind of how I am now—just aimlessly blowing around.

Is there nothing noble to be found in what I'm doing?

Where is the passion, the beauty? What is to become of me, this lonely wanderer through life's dark corridors? I can't believe that life is such a tragic occurrence. Somewhere is peace, is beauty and joy.

Laughter feels a million miles away; understanding feels a billion miles away. And I, a trillion.

· · · · · · ·

After session:

A very interesting session. Went in, not wanting to talk, feeling overwhelmed, hypersensitive, wanting to hide. Cried a little, kept getting younger and smaller, very thought-empty and wordless.

Snuggled up against the floor, feeling the hum of the building against my body, my mind empty, all sensation. It felt so wonderful, being a little baby with no thoughts or worries, just being warm and sleepy—so I slept. Felt much less diffuse after waking.

Strange, huh?

· · · · · · ·

Amazing, I go to Rick's Restaurant, and I write in my journal, "J'ai besoin d'une femme." So a pretty young redhead sitting across the room sends me a note saying, "I want you." Of course, my ego goes sky-rocketing through the roof, and my integrity drops through the floor. How can I look this gift horse in the mouth?

Integrity is a big question these days—mine anyway. Am I so in need of acceptance that I will give myself to a strange woman?

My landmark is Primal Therapy, of course. That is why I'm here, and everything else is done in service to that.

This is the idea anyway. But it's hard to know what's best for this. Sleeping or not sleeping, fasting or not, drinking or not, thinking or not, daydreaming of Marie or not, running or not, worrying or not. God, what confusion.

Do what feels best, right?

Bullshit, nothing and yet everything feels best. At this rate, it'll take me decades to get clear. But I just can't move any quicker.

Or can I?

. . . .

All this writing seems stupid; all this waiting seems stupid too. Nothing is happening. Paul does not want to change badly enough to confront himself.

I have been craving women lately in a way never before felt. It's not so much lust—though there is a powerful, and not very clear, sexual desire running through me.

It feels very immature, compulsive. I call women I know; I call women I don't know; I invite strange women to the house, not knowing why. I even tried to call Marie, not really wanting to talk to her—just somehow to let her feel my presence.

By accident, I found Cindy was in town. Excited, I called her, but she was very wary, distant, on guard, afraid. I was hurt, but perhaps it's best. Maybe I just need to be totally alone.

. . . .

Ahh, a very fine day indeed, full of different things.

First, woke up early, in the arms of a very lovely young woman: fresh, exciting, flaming red hair, soft white skin . . . . It was a nice encounter, a sort of test, to spend time with a stranger and try to be real. Dancing, drinking, flirting, talking and talking, testing the limits of honesty. Letting myself feel good, making her feel good and free to reveal herself.

Then went into session very sleepy, hung-over. Without much resistance or force, I delicately slipped into some stuff, and got a soft glimpse of life in the womb, and of slowly sliding out. Felt the torrential loneliness of that first, great, inexplicable separation—that first acknowledgment of the experience of being an individual in a world of individuals, having to let go of that heavenly autonomous connection to the whole. Such sadness.

And the insights were profound: about loneliness, communication, the need for others, aloneness and connectedness.

My most powerful, penetrating experience in therapy to date.

. . . .

Another very interesting day, not pleasant or graceful, but full of potency. Session was rough—struggling with deep, maybe the deepest, of my unresolved feelings. Toxic, give-up, death kinds of things, that (though just barely touched on) left me in a horrible physical state: aches, cellular aches, extreme disorientation, poisonousness, anguish and helpless hopelessness, fear. Give-up fear; not run-for-your-life fear, but just lie-down-and-die fear.

Followed by intense anxiety over Marie. Anger, resentment, hate. I felt my love for her just washed away by my anger, my envy, my hurt. Calling her every ugly name in the book, cursing, slandering, belittling. Feeling stupid with the intensity of my needs for her; foolish in my actions, embarrassed by our whole affair. It feels like I can almost let her go now. But I must make sure it is resolved within, and not merely cut off. It will take time, but I think our connection is fading. Is this a blessing or a tragedy, I wonder? Such a loss.

And then Cindy called. She doesn't seem to have changed. Still locked into her smiley little world where "having fun is all that counts." I felt a little more capable of tolerating it, accepting it, appreciating it. But I still got those twinges when she'd laugh or say some familiar phrase, and I still felt a real warmth for her.

She will never understand who I am or what I'm doing, though. Who will, huh? Of course, I compare every woman with Marie, and none even comes close to measuring up.

I guess things are going well. I'm baffled. Only time will tell. I hope. On and on I pick my way.

. . . .

If I can get somewhat stabilized in my situation here, the feelings will come easier, the old patterns will reassert themselves. Now, though, things are too vague, in between, undefined. It feels like some bizarre vacation. I need to let go of Santa Cruz, and commit myself to . . . ? It's not possible to work toward the future yet, meaning a return to Santa Cruz and school. That just avoids the immediate confrontation. Perhaps it will still be there when I surface from this deep pool of self-exploration.

But this is my life now; I am working on being Paul, not a better lover for Marie, or an aspiring architect. Slowly Santa Cruz fades from my thoughts. That doesn't mean I have to give up what I learned there, but I can't realistically define my future; that's all.

It will form itself.

. . . .

Slowly, now, things begin to accelerate. My home becomes established, I start defining my parameters—my existence in this city. It will be an isolated one; I have the freedom to choose whatever friendship comes along. The days seem always shorter than I have need of, so I acknowledge that my priority here is my relationship with myself.

. . . .

Hello Dad,

Balmy, breezy day, the sky awash with this grey cloud, rain over the mountains. On the other side lies Pagosa and you, and further on, Santa Cruz and the ocean. There is always a strong pull from the west. The city is quiet, except for the constant roar of the jets, which I never grow used to. I sit in the sun, listen to music, prepare meals, come and go from work.

Life passes by me, in constant motion. I feel stranded on my little island of Paul. Change is slow: after nearly two months I feel only the tiniest subtle hints of difference. Perhaps that is good. I might choose to view that as a sign that the changes are working deep, beyond my conscious comprehension. I don't try too hard anymore. Futility and frustration never were very comfort-

ing companions. Surrender frees me from responsibility—and guilt. I now have weekly sessions, instead of the more frequent ones earlier.

Working a lot these days: five nights per week at the restaurant. (It's a good excuse for a bike ride, anyway.) And, tomorrow, I begin working days, next door—helping to build a new house. Free time is spent playing in my little garden. A few new friendships just beginning to form, but most of my time is spent alone, crowded together with all of my ghosts. We're getting to know each other a little.

A big hug,
Paul

Dear Paul,

A shopping day, bright and calm, in Durango; I'm watching the river tumble muddily past me here in the spot you and I used to visit together. A nice change of setting for me—but by tonight I'll be glad to return to my solitude on Turkey Springs Road. God, this is really a fine part of the world, que no?

I'm thinking of you often, but haven't been in a writing mood, and seem to keep quite busy this time of year. Hearing of your progress (including both ups and downs) in your letters and phone calls is ex-

*tremely interesting and rewarding to me. Sounds like you've made a fine
start, and I'm relieved. But it's never easy, is it?*

*Leslie's visit was beautiful; she and I grow closer all the time. I have
nothing but admiration for her, and for you. My two best friends. Know
that you have my constant love and support.*

Dad

Once again, it grows late, and sleep eludes me. Deep feelings I
cannot grasp are humming in each cell of my body. Feelings so profound and intense, I feel that if I were to open the gates and let the
flood flow out, it would be the end. Perhaps that is what happens to
people who suddenly and inexplicably die in their sleep. With no
mechanisms working for filtering the flow of understanding, the truth
swoops out of the sky like a giant fireball, enveloping the mind in an
overwhelming flash of wisdom.

I cannot know these things, but I sense them. It is the *intent*,
searching for its *content*; it is a void, waiting to be filled; it is an idea,
craving form.

My sleeplessness is an anxiety, a resistance to some truth reaching for recognition, a truth which slips in as I sleep, like some phan-
tom lover who takes me when I am open and child-like. I have some
sense of what happens when one is asleep, the workings of the mind
unhampered by consciousness. Why then do I fear it? It can only lead
to further clarity and a more clearly recognized reality. Is it so painful,
I wonder?

. . . .

Almost summer; gentle afternoon rains, numinous sunsets, birds
in fresh form and sprouts in the garden.

Life begins to resemble a routine, a routine I do not trust, nor
welcome. When things around me are new and untried, I feel a
power—a potential for change and liveliness. But when I surround
myself with patterns, my own well-worn and caustic patterns assert
themselves too, and I am once again, unavoidably, the Paul I detest to
be. Inane, insecure, compulsive, bland, lethargic, worrisome, contracted.

How will I ever change?

. . . .

Spent the evening with my new friend, Susan. A very different woman: sensitive, soft, easy, very sensual, athletic, voluptuous. It's wonderful to encounter such people, with no effort—people so easy to be with, to touch, to talk to, to accept.

Sally's been in town too. Never have I experienced such sexuality with an older woman like this. How it brings out the little boy, excited and afraid. Even in my childishness, a powerful sexuality shines through that is so surprising. Women far beyond me reach out to me with their eyes, their movement, their odor.

. . . .

Hi Dad,

Afternoon, sitting at a little outdoor café where I often stop to drink wine on my way to work. My life at work is so different than my life at not-work, that it usually is a good idea to make some type of distinct transition, preparation. I would be a real basket case if I went to work aux naturale, so a little wine or caffeine, some peripheral humanity, some urban exposure usually helps ease the shock.

I sense myself approaching some vortex in my therapy that I've encountered so many times before, and have never been able to break through. I can be assured of some very painful days ahead. Maybe this time I can finally slice through to the other side, with some help and my new tools to pound away with.

Thank God I've some stability in my outside life right now. I know from experience that I will have little energy to expend on the more practical side of survival. The world will have to do without my help for a while. I doubt it will notice.

Subtle changes continue to appear, apparent only in my most sensitive moments. Quite frankly, I still can't see much possibility of success, but there is some hope, sometimes. It's a strange life I find myself in. Certainly not one that I would've chosen, if I'd been given the chance.

Paul

Dear Paul,

My life goes on here—probably much more calmly and predictably than yours does there. I wonder how your therapy—your inner responses—would be different if your setting could be as pristine and tranquil as this one? Well that's only an impossible dream. But in an ideal world, I would prefer that all such crucial activities take place away from the horror of the city—out where there is still something natural.

On the other hand, sometimes exterior discomforts will serve to trigger more important inner sources of the old pain, as you have observed—so it isn't all bad.

I'm impressed with how well you are able to keep the pragmatic sides of your life under control—along with the demands of your therapy in Denver. My compliments, and

> *Love,*
> *Dad*

Sunday afternoon, quiet as this city ever gets. Becalmed on a sea of emotional doldrums, adrift in a little boat, without comfort, without oars, waiting for the monsoon winds to blow me home—or blow me apart.

It's a funny life that leads me now. Slightly tainted with meaning, my torn and yellowing pages stained with pain and question, growing brittle. Am I dying?

It feels like it. My body such an uncomfortable place to be: aching and toxic and bent out of shape, listless and lethargic. Nothing works too well right now, neither mind nor body nor heart. Resigning myself to forces I cannot define, I continue to descend. Wondering if I will be born again, or if my disintegration will be complete, with nothing left alive to take root and sprout anew.

Destined or doomed?

. . . .

Dad,

Tough times; screamingly empty days, sleepless terror at night. My life seems a poisoned process, inexplicable torture from all sides, inside and out.

144

Some spend their time on earth among the clouds. Mine seems destined for perpetual descent into the dank dark contracted bowels of fear, dangling over the depths by a single fragile thread. Wrapped around my neck; my salvation and yet my destruction. What's the phrase? *A bad egg. There lies my bitter secret.*

A bad egg; how poignantly those simple words can explain it all, to one who is sensitive enough to grasp the incredible implications. And the tragedy.

I'm tired, Dad. I don't know what's to become of me. I need to come visit soon.

Paul

I called Paul in Denver and urged him to come to me as soon as he could. A week or two later, he did, and I guess it helped—some. But it was obvious that he had a long way ahead of him yet to traverse.

Dad,

Well, back in Denver, deathly Denver, pressing in on me like a vise, robbing me of breath and injecting me with its subtle, ubiquitous toxins. There is nothing here but struggle. It fills the air, petrifies bodies. Weary eyes glazed with terror stare past me wherever I go, sapping my strength. I cannot stay here much longer. There is no way to resist the deadness that pervades this evil place. And I cannot resist, nor resolve, the brutal struggle of those around me; they all suck the life from my body. We all share this vacuum of pain.

Have I really changed Dad? Can I ever catch up with my life?

Thanks for sharing so much of yourself. If only you and I were alone in the world. Yes?

I love you,
Paul

· · · · · · ·

Denver continues to try my patience; the therapy is too slow, too careful. I need to be slapped in the face, run down and broken apart. Only acute pain makes me feel at all alive. I can acknowledge the potential power of Primal Therapy, but I cannot commit myself. I am

145

always on the outside looking in. Perhaps if I turn and look behind me?

Tragic irony.

. . . .

Nearing Christmas, well into the season of loneliness and mortal, conscious despair. What is it about the holidays that presents us with the unavoidable realization that we are all alone—desperately alone? Is it the reminder of times past, of awkward, incomprehensible en-counters with unexpected emptiness?

All around me are people reaching out, reaching out to unfath-omable voids. Crying out to be reassured that they are loved, that they are real, that they exist somewhere outside of their own minds.

. . . .

Hello Dad,

Just killing time before work, sitting in a tiny French café, drink-ing wine and smoking cigarettes, sustaining the sick life of a desperate waiter.

The times before I need to be somewhere are always anxious ones for me, especially if they are new and unknown, and even more so if they are somehow involved with my struggle to survive. So the hours before a shift at Zach's Restaurant, at least for now, are tense and frightening.

It's still too early to say how the job at Zach's will work out. There's a great deal of relief at seeing some money coming in once again. And a great deal of sorrow and disappointment at the strange and senseless method for doing so. You can imagine the sensorial confusion after eight hours of work in a very busy, loud restaurant, dishing out hundreds of dollars of food to face after strange face—everything moving so rapidly, so desperately.

Due to a problem with scheduling, I will have to miss my therapy session this week. I can feel my body gearing up for its weekly release, and it scares me to know that that pressure will have to be held back (in) for another week.

It's cold, grey and windy here. People are scurrying around like frightened bloodless bugs, desperately seeking safety from the open empty spaces.

I've been almost a year in Denver now. It still seems like it's doing more harm than good. What's the alternative though, I wonder?

Love,
Paul

Dear Paul,

We're snugly home today, with a beautiful snowfall in progress; wintertime here is a special kind of magic, as you know. I feel like getting a note ready for you—not knowing when it can be mailed. Fortunately, we got all our away-from-home errands done yesterday, so the snow brings no pressure—only pleasure.

So you're nearly a year into your very demanding undertaking. What a massive commitment for you to have made. I still believe you'll be glad you did. Just hang in—I'm confident you have what it takes to succeed with this.

I really do intend to come to Denver in the next few weeks. Don't give up on me. I'm awfully eager to see you.

Love,
Dad

Spring begins to return to Denver, and with it, some of the pressure inside me is eased, siphoned off, dissipated by my increased physical activity. The world outside becomes sensorially more tolerable, and I can once again turn my gaze outward.

Either way I look though, in or out, the view is ultimately unacceptable, and I am still trapped in a world of anxious lifelessness. The therapy is taking hold, but so slowly. I feel like there is an ocean of cold, lifeless water to swim through, and I have yet to crest those first giant waves that are crashing in upon my shores.

Will the open sea swallow me, or guide me home? What lies on those distant shores? And what lies waiting for me in the depths below?

Somehow begins to blossom a fresh and painful and tragic understanding of my inevitable mortality. A respect and fear of life, that is fed by my own desperate craving to someday be alive.

Those distant shores, that beckon, unknown.

. . . .

Sitting out beneath the clouds of a
soft, damp spring night.
Without a mind of my own,
without a dream to lead me on.
Only frustration.
The mortal frustration of a being
whose mind can tap into the
limitless universe of imagination,
and knowledge beyond my powers
to exercise.
Man the everlack.
Perpetrator of the almost,
and the never quite enough.

. . . .

Today I have been in Denver a year, the time I allocated to myself
as a commitment to not run away. So stop and look at what I'm doing
here now, is it right, is it worth being alive for, is there a better choice,
are there any other choices?

I am tempted to define, to defend, and to plan ahead. But all that
is based on the premise that I contain some willful power with which
to deliberate the course of my self. I certainly feel no such power. And
Primal Therapy has confused me as to whether my responses (healthy
or not) to my situation are really very accurate gauges with which to
judge the appropriateness of my actions. Can I truly accept that all of
my self-abuse is necessary, is actually leading me toward health? Am I
resigned to resignation?

I know that I cannot stay in Denver much longer. How do I
know when to leave? When I have the key to Primal, when I can access
myself without the help of my therapists. Then it will be the time to
move on.

But how long, I wonder, until then?

One year of it behind him. How had it gone? The intensity of many of his reliving experiences, the wonder at the mass of information recorded internally in a single individual; it all filled him with awe, and also with mixed feelings, from time to time, about his progress. It would be two more months before his journal reflected any significant optimism.

. . . .

Dear Paul,

I'm out in the woods again today, filling my journal with feelings, questions, observations, analyses—of myself. Words. Ninety-nine percent worthless, I expect. Wish there was a gem of truth, of wisdom in there somewhere. I have a persistent response to my trying to capture something of my insides for you in a letter: I think I would prefer to tell you how it's been for the past several weeks, maybe. But I end up saying how I feel this moment, only. And I imagine you perceiving this as a longer-term picture. Maybe—maybe not. I guess when I try to transmit my real feeling, that it just automatically gets an immediacy to it; it's not a chronicle of Chuck's most recent one month history. It's the best I can do.

I think that these few days of conscientious searching inside myself, and setting aside some of my usual occupations, is going to be good. So far, anyway. A couple of months ago I felt I really got down to some kind of bedrock—and it still feels pretty accurate. I wrote: the only really important question is: what am I really afraid of? Deep inside myself?

Outside, in my surroundings, things look good. Spring is here. My stained glass piece is ready to submit to the art show. In a week or so I'll start to shape a large pile of gorgeous cherrywood out in the shop into possibly my most ambitious piece of woodwork yet: the desk. I'm very excited about that. We had a great couple of days in Albuquerque, choosing the wood.

I'm about out for now. Perhaps I'll feel like writing again soon. Hope there'll be an opportunity to see you before long. It always means an awful lot to me. Better than spending time with anyone else I've ever known.

I love you.

Dad

My heaviness continues to grow. I guess it doesn't really get any heavier, or larger. It just feels like it, as my body gets more and more weary from carrying it around, and it demands more and more of my attention in dealing with it.

Every once in a while I set my burden down and try chiseling away at it, instead of carrying it around all the time. I've managed to reduce it by a few little piles of dust, left behind to mark my trail, or maybe to blow away in the breeze.

Sitting in silence
staring off into space,
staring hard.
Through the soft blossoms of the apple tree
beyond the heavy grey clouds in the sky.
My gaze penetrates nothing
because it comes from nowhere—
save the depths of a cold grey heart,
heavier and emptier than the spring skies.
More fragile than any blossom,
waiting to spring into life.
Yet fading all the while.

Joy, Beauty, Sadness, Love

The Twenty-eighth Year

After weeks of apathy, frustration, nothing being accomplished in therapy sessions—shallow comprehensions and circular patterns of thought, becoming angry and despairing of forward motion; a new pattern begins to emerge, a new hidden pocket of myself which I have never acknowledged, but which I have lived my life around. Working with Vince now to accommodate the shift in my focus, my emerging understanding and uncoverings.

Perhaps I've released enough very early stuff in my therapy to make room for, to learn a tolerance and trust which allows for, the shaky appearance of later childhood insight. A very, very frightening thing for me to face. That early infant stuff was easy, spontaneous, somewhat passive, almost anonymous. The discomforts were mainly physical: lethargy, aches and pains, druggedness. The pressure not so acute.

Now, realizing my imminent confrontation with my childhood pain throws me into a state of rigid panic. I'm afraid that to feel these things will be much more sharply painful, my reality more shaken, my discomfort of an emotional and cognitive type. I can expect an ordeal of ineptness, incompetence, awkwardness, night-time trauma, jealousy, resentment of authority, perhaps speech problems, etc.

And sessions will take much more effort, assertive action, and queasy persistence, against my maze of defenses which are protecting me from the truth. I do not want to remember my life as a little boy.

I can sense the agony already, beginning to push.

. . . .

Hello Dad,

Moving on toward dusk here after a dreary, drizzly day in Denver. Days like this make me realize how vulnerable I am to the general mood of the people around me. Waiting at Zach's restaurant on fifty or sixty business people who arrive irritated by the weather, a week of suffering at their toxic jobs in downtown Denver, and whatever other dishonest pain they need to slough off on me, their servant, has a profound impact on me and my own inside situation. Though I realize that they can only remind me of feelings I already carry inside, it is still disquieting to acknowledge that I am so at the mercy of others. Their anger and fear seems like it is constantly polluting my struggles to come to a pure and specific confrontation with my own pain, the only thing that has any value to me right now. My feelings are inevitably diluted by those of the people around me.

No wonder I crave solitude so much. It isn't so much a reaction to the noise, smoke, and smells, but a need inside crying out to pay attention to the emerging feelings which I attend to so half-heartedly. It causes me to despair that I'll ever come to terms with myself.

One thing Primal Therapy has moved me to accept is how huge a task I have before me before I can ever believe that life is worth living. I doubt that I could adequately convey to anyone the profound sense of hopelessness, helplessness, and unworthiness which weighs me down so heavily.

As an afterthought, it occurs to me that powerlessness is the father of all these feelings, the real feeling to be encountered, yet one that seems so beyond my reach. I feel that there is very little possibility of ever bringing my intentions and my capabilities into synch. How long must I endure such emptiness?

As I ponder this question, I come to realize that the feeling is one of nearly absolute starvation. There is virtually no nourishment, no motivation, no something-that-is-imperative-to-my-survival and which I can't produce (shouldn't have to produce) myself, coming to me from the outside world.

I sit like an old car in a vacant lot, rusting away. The difference is that I am alive, and can't wait. And like a body fasting, without subsistence from the outside, I will use up my limited store of reserves, and literally eat myself up from the inside out, in order to survive just a little longer.

So I remain in Denver, rationing my meager supplies of life-giving-substance and wonder how long, if ever, until reinforcements arrive?

Fascinating, how I can sit here and let this shit just burble out. It almost sounds eloquent. Yet it feels so bad. It's about as connected as masturbation is to procreation. A pretty feeble gesture . . . .

Yet somewhere in the spontaneous occurrence of these words is some wisdom, some growth. Not nearly enough, though. Nowhere near enough.

Me

Dear Paul,

Yes, somewhere in the spontaneous occurrence of your painful words appears some new wisdom—some additional growth. I know it seems so little sometimes, that it can never come fast enough to ever catch up.

I can't predict your path; I can't, in conscience, assure you that you are very near the threshold of a glorious breakthrough. I do look and listen closely to what I see and hear in you of late—pain and all—and I'm gratified at your advance.

You've certainly earned everything you accomplish, and you have my undying love and support.

Dad

· · · · · · ·

At home, my second marriage was not surviving well, and I had serious doubts about its future—but it didn't seem prudent to add this to all that was going on in Paul's life right then. He certainly had his hands full.

153

Insights emerge increasingly now, inside and outside of sessions. I'm more able to distinguish between present aches, pains, and attitudes, and those prototypical responses which are slowly but surely emerging. This awareness gives me a more deliberate access to confrontations, and because of this the therapy should move along more quickly as I gain more choice in the manner and time in which I submerge myself in my feelings. I am gaining the power of focus. I feel very lucky that all my emphasis is on birth. I can get right to the heart of things, and the changes will be much more intense.

Feelings are much easier to get into, and much harder to stop, and though the depth is not there yet, the momentum is increasing. I can now sustain a feeling sometimes for one or two hours, rising from it and then submerging myself in it repeatedly.

I grow closer to the truth.

· · · · · · ·

Outside of Dad's now, late of a cool dry evening—the house to myself for a while. The stillness is profound, reaching into me—calm after a week of quiet, mountains, motion, and some bittersweet solitude.

Able to quiet my mind a bit, and peer beyond the chatter to the fragile and restless stirrings inside, waiting to take form and be recognized.

· · · · · · ·

Early fall: still warm, but dry and suffocating, the air too heavy with emptiness. Life drains slowly from the world, leaving me to struggle along with my own meager spirit.

My new lover, Jane, excites me—but seems, somehow, to be almost too much to try to integrate right now. Her recent departure for her European trip leaves me alone, in a state of mortal exhaustion. Too weary to resist, that old grey fog of despair begins to seep through my widening cracks. It's going to be a very rough winter. Ominous signs of overwhelming sadness appear on my horizons.

I am too weak to avoid it. Perhaps that is good. But the dam that holds back my fear begins to erode, rapidly now, and if I had need to erect such a massive, complex structure, then the volume of fear which it holds inside must be awesome.

How to bear the onslaught? I am filled with foreboding. Yet I must risk the relief of release, for I can no longer maintain the tremendous forces within. To continue to resist would mean a long, ugly, and painful death.

Better to brave the fury, of . . . ?

· · · · · · ·

These warm fall afternoons I spend basking alone in the sun, languishing in my rare moments of peace. Anxiety is a steady drone, and it takes the distraction of books, drugs, compulsive planning and replanning to keep it at a tolerable level. Not the most graceful solution, but seemingly the best I can do.

Relief at having Jane gone, and intense apprehension about her return. Hoping fervently she will be gone many months and give us time to separately resolve some stuff. An early return would throw me into unbearable confusion.

Craving some female company, but feeling no sense of desperation that might lead me into an uncomfortable situation. My solitude is more important right now. I can wait.

Starting once again to feel some progress in therapy. I can no longer just coast along; I must spend more time, at home, at work, everywhere, trying to feel. I have wasted so much time already.

Financially, I am committed to suffering existence in Denver for another year. I hope I can make the most of it. I hope I can somehow learn to tolerate Zach's Restaurant with less damage done, for I doubt that a better situation will present itself.

Feeling fairly clear today. Some irritating details of my life are finding resolution, and I can relax, at least a little.

And tomorrow?

· · · · · · ·

This tomorrow is not so clear. Choosing to spend my time alone on a cloudy Saturday afternoon. Never very comfortable alone, but more acceptable than my awkwardness with people. With Jane gone,

I more fully recognize my lack of spirit, my subduedness, my ugly passivity. A very basic pattern in my life has always been to team up with very dynamic women, life-of-the-party types who know how to charm people, to have fun at any time, in any situation, and who make up for my depressing lack of charisma.

I suppose there's nothing wrong in choosing a partner who compensates for my inadequacy, but still, it feels dishonest. If I can't make it on my own, I shan't make it at all: a very important issue. Tears accompany my overwhelming sense of failure. I can't imagine living another fifty years with these feelings; I can't imagine living another five.

. . . .

The first snows of winter fell yesterday, a discouraging reminder of what lies ahead. As usual, I resist it totally, as I resist everything, accepting it only as another burden to bear, another excuse with which to flaunt my anxiety.

I continue to probe my fears tangentially, skimming the surface, rather than penetrating to the heart. My involvement is still in clumsily coping with the *symptoms* of my pain, and not its essence. I need to refocus on my therapy. It's not a very good reason for living, but for lack of other goals, it's all that I've got. I need to reevaluate my present situation, my behavior and needs, in terms of implicit feelings—not on any outer reality.

It had been an intense and confusing time for my son. I knew that he was reaching for that essential feeling of rightness. But it continued to be a difficult journey. Then, about eighteen months after leaving Santa Cruz to begin therapy, Paul made a short visit back. It was a brief ten-day return to his California haunts; the experiences there were deeply felt.

Mill Valley, California: exhausted after two days of driving, the tension of high speed, bad weather, sitting too long, worries about the car, cocaine. Overwhelmed by the emotions involved with being with Andy, spending time with strangers, seeing the ocean again.

The stormy, violent weather is appropriate to the feelings involved with my being here. The storms are raging within as well as without, with an occasional break in the clouds to warm my weary bones.

If I can keep from being totally overloaded by the feelings brought up by being here, if I can keep my safety valves clean and functioning properly, so that I don't feel too much too soon and just shut down—then this trip may prove to be the trigger that propels me through the vortex of my fears and, finally, out into the wide open spaces of my deepest and truest feelings.

· · · · · · ·

Santa Cruz now: sitting in the late afternoon sun on the rocks above Woodrow Beach, a place of overwhelming implication, a reminder of an incident so humiliating that I am unable to put it into words. My first thought at surveying the scene of that tragic night is a sense of the incredulous. My struggle to live that night, the innate, irrepressible, physical struggle to live, was so powerful, so rawly prototypical.

Being in Santa Cruz has forced me deep within my body—my essence. Whereas my time in Mill Valley was spent wrestling with a cognitive confusion, Santa Cruz has touched me at a deeper, purer level of physical reaction. I can sense an overwhelming of my capacity to fully experience, to integrate being here.

I am calmer than I expected to be, but also strangely restless, in a way that implies my inability to connect with an environment too packed with meaning for me. But my innate sense of limitation is protecting me well. I hope that enough fresh material is being stirred up so that I can return to my therapy in Colorado and deal with it in earnest, to break the haze of inertia in which I've been floundering these past months.

· · · · · · ·

Just met with Marie. Jesus fucking Christ!

Talk about a complex, intense encounter. Two articulate people, dumbfounded by being in each other's presence again, delicately trying to engage—not knowing where to start, how much to say, not trusting ourselves or each other, because the feelings and fear and pain have never subsided. And the magnitude of our connection still so apparent.

Marie was very closed, apprehensive, defensive in her particularly aggressive way. Holding on tight to the ways in which she protects herself. I am so surprised that she sought me out, that she instigated the encounter, that she even wanted to see me. The whole thing is so clumsy and confusing, yet seemingly so important.

I can easily recognize now how completely opposite Jane and Marie are. Even in physical appearance. Jane is tall, dark, slim, likes to dress up and be noticed. Marie is short, blond, voluptuous, dresses down, and likes to be physically anonymous.

Jane is impulsive, indecisive, always wanting to have fun, extremely sexual, warm, feminine, disorganized, giving, and physically oriented. Expansive, brightly colored, explosive.

Marie is controlled, decisive, dogmatic, a workaholic, cold, masculine, compulsively organized, selfish, mentally oriented, contracted, shades of blues and greys, implosive.

They are both dynamic, aggressive women, oriented toward men, angry at their fathers, complex, unusually mature, and unique! Both are little girls, and both very much women. The obvious correlation is that I escaped from Marie through Jane. And reading the descriptions above makes Jane a much more attractive person to be with. Why did I so desperately love Marie, and why so much trepidation with Jane?

I love women. If I am capable of anything, it is to love. And that is a rare and undeniable gift—and a power to recognize. With delight!

· · · · · · ·

Lunch with Marie today. It was surprisingly easy. In contrast to yesterday, she dropped her guard, for the most part, and we were able to talk: about the past, the present, the future.

It showed me how much I've changed—I've grown. Even talking of the past, talking about some very painful episodes I thought we'd be best to avoid, I was able to remain clear, detached but engaged, confident of my ideas and feelings, and able to accept Marie's without defensiveness, even when she became angry, a situation which two years ago would have become awkward and ugly.

I think she was surprised, and delighted. She began to open up in a very direct way, talking of her relationships, of her loneliness. She's reaching out to me in a way I wouldn't have dreamed possible. It's obvious she still loves me a great deal.

I'm still baffled by that, and still intimidated by her intensity. She is very self-contained, a professional architect now, and she will be enormously successful. She's got the world in the palm of her hand, I expect.

I still wonder what I have to offer her, how I could possibly keep up with or challenge such a woman. But that's not really very important right now, because I don't have to. I'm leaving tomorrow, and all that matters now is to enjoy the warmth and love that we feel for each other.

· · · · · · ·

The world is being very kind to me right now, and things are working out much better than I could have imagined. And, of course, I get scared when things work out right, because I am used to failure. I can't trust success. Somewhere along the line I learned that failure is inevitable for me; I expect defeat, I expect the world to turn against me, to turn on me if I give in to the natural inclination to trust.

And so I create my own failure, so at least *that* is in my own control.

· · · · · · ·

The changes in me are hard to describe, hard even to recognize. Surely I have let go of lots of inappropriate anxiety. I feel less like I've actually cleared anything specific inside, but more like I've *gained the tools* for dealing with my feelings. I'm more capable of recognizing potentially ugly situations; I've gained that little bit of extra time, before I'm sucked into a reaction, to be able to (at the very least) close down and back off before being swept away. I've gained that choice.

So now the question is, now that I can fully trust my involvement with Primal Therapy, how to maximize this endeavor, and how to judge the time when I can leave Denver, change my focus to more worldly things, and carry on by myself.

It certainly will be a most unusual life that I will create for myself. But I've got a long way to go still, before I am willing to commit myself to life. I am capable of experiencing only such a small percentage of what might be available to me.

But, imagine: a person such as Marie can still love me, not only a very intensely motivated and successful person, but more importantly, a person who so quickly can shut out the reality I present. In other words, she has to risk an incredible amount to open up to me, and still she feels it worth her while.

I must have something important to offer; there must be some beauty I contain that other people would like to experience.

. . . .

Ely, Nevada; fighting the winds, rain, snow and long miles back to Colorado. Oscillating between the silliness of hours on the road and the great melancholy of being alone with my thoughts.

It was very hard to leave California. I leave behind so many people important to me. It felt as much like home as any that I have had; not in regard to a house to live in, or a job, but rather an atmosphere, an environment very resonant with my interior landscape. Santa Cruz is calling to me to come back. I wonder why?

Spent my last night with Marie; tried to keep it light and playful. Found myself phasing in and out of love with her throughout the night. She's a very strange person. I can say that I love her, though, without any particular need to be with her. In fact, I'd rather not right now. It's enough to know that she cares—in her strange and complex way.

She's changed an awful lot. In part because her sublimation has taken new forms, and in part because she's loosening up. We had fun drinking, fun talking, fun fucking. She's opened up incredibly to her sexual capabilities. Her body is full and delicious. I sensed a new need for her to dominate and captivate men; undoubtedly she's been seeing a lot of men, but somehow that doesn't bother me. It was enough to hold her in my arms again, to lie deep and long within her.

So, Marie lies behind me, and Jane before me, soon to arrive back in Denver. Is my excitement only lust, or do I truly miss her? I miss her—I know that.

It should be interesting, and fun. I hope I never lose my delight and infatuation with women!

. . . .

Another volume of my journal draws to an end. What a strange, strange period of my life. I could reflect endlessly on what it all means. My time in Denver, despite the ugliness and awkwardness of my daily existence, certainly marks the beginning of my coming of age—of acceptance into the circle of life.

So much has opened up the past few weeks. The awareness of enjoyment and adventure as a basis for living. Finally sensing what it means to leave the pain behind. Miraculously, the first vivacious sprouts of a love of myself.

The recent focus of Primal Therapy has been to reverse the projection of my anger, doubt, mistrust, hostility, unreality away from myself—releasing an awesome burden that has been exhausting me. With confidence comes a new clarity, calmness—a subtle sense of the implications of a potential purpose to my life.

The pursuit of satisfaction.

The experience of joy.

The beauty and sadness of love.

About this time, I found myself terminating my second fifteen-year marriage, leaving my reclusive home in the deep, still forest, and returning to Denver for a time. This made it possible to again arrange to live with Paul—for the next year: a precious opportunity. He was at a point in his quest which was highly interesting and rewarding to me. I hope that it was mostly helpful to him, as well, to be near me, but I can't be sure. At any rate, he continued to give it his all.

We compared our experiences in Primal Therapy now and then, and often came up against the familiar inability to make very thoughtful expressions with words—of the feelings we had each encountered. But, even so, we were each probably the best listener available anywhere for the other's attempts to explain. It was a special time, containing pain as well as progress. A period of bringing us even closer together than before. But not always easy.

Exhausted, and it's late, but the day won't free its grip on me yet. Exhausted to the point of severe melancholy. With no strength left for resistance, my insides well up in me like a flood, saturating my being with feelings too powerful to ignore, yet too frightening to confront.

So much has happened in the past few weeks: my trip to California, new communications with Marie, Jane's return, the holidays, Dad moving here. I'm surprised I'm still on my feet.

I wish I could loose these feelings and have done with it, and rid my body of its discomfort. But I sense that this may be a real treasure from my Pandora's box, waiting for release, and that the intensity of my fears needs to build to a crescendo in order to break through my barriers.

· · · · · · ·

Now I ponder what to do about Jane. So many conflicting emotions writhing inside of me. Terrible feelings of guilt, abandoning her in a period of great need. The threat of terrible loneliness and the heartache of loss, perhaps unnecessarily. Why do I feel the need to turn away from another's love? Is it because she's just not quite right for me?

Is it some manifestation of a primal feeling that causes me to pull away from everyone? Is it punishment stemming from my self-hate? Am I in some bizarre fashion trying to reverse the role I played with Marie?

Again, I can't distinguish the past from the present. And I am so far away from myself. Like a picture out of focus, my being split into a thousand images, waiting to be drawn together into one clear person. Instead, the movement is opposite. I continue to fracture, to fraction, to dissipate into smaller and disparate pieces.

Perhaps I am just feeling my own mortality. As I lie here in bed, and slowly turn into dust.

Paul's affair with Jane did come to an end; with all of the inner attention and inner turmoil added to the pressures of his external life, it

was just too much to try to deal with. He missed her from time to time,
but never again sought to reestablish their connection.

One o'clock in the morning, the first day of a brand new year. So
tired. High on cocaine and alcohol—my system surging with anxiety.
No big deal, I guess—ushering in a new year. Except that it gives me
pause to stop and think about where I'm at, what I'm doing. And,
maybe, what lies ahead.

I'm still here. I've survived in spite of the momentous struggle
taking place. Life is so harsh and brutal; yet I continue to exist.

And there is a chance that things might go very nicely in the
future. The potential is there.

· · · · · · ·

A fine sunny day, seated on a bench in Washington Park. The
first really warm day in a while. Good weather makes me think of the
future. It inspires an urge to make plans.

I feel the need to define what it is I really want to be doing with
myself. Perhaps if I could be more specific, I would have the extra
power to make things happen. I grow tired of this endless discomfort
of feeling at the mercy of my circumstances. It seems that all of my
free time is spent in recovering from the agony and abuse at Zach's.
I'm never able to catch up; there's never any extra energy for growth;
it seems all I am able to do is maintain—to endure.

But there needs to be more to my being alive than simple en-
durance.

What is it that I require for myself?
- lots of time and a peaceful place for contemplation.
- easy access to adventure, meaning a physical interaction with
  the environment.
- sensitive people to share with.
- time and energy to create.
- some very specific study.
- a means of support which allows me the freedom, in time and
  energy, to pursue these things—a means which allows me to
  save—and a type of work that is in some way satisfying.

• the time and money to do my therapy more deliberately.

Yet how can I reach for the future when I am still so wrapped up in the past? It feels like, with the modest degree of progress that I've made in therapy, that I could spend my whole life catching up with the present. And then where would I be? How would I feel on my deathbed? Is that what is meant by: a man dies when he can, and not when he should?

It's not easy striving for a life of beauty. And I have yet to earn my self-respect.

· · · · · · ·

I stare at myself in the mirror, and find no communication with what I see. I am a stranger to myself, unable to connect with my reflection; there is no current of understanding being reflected in, nor reflected out. There seems no being inside capable of projection or perception.

My image is vague, transient, and contorted. The eyes bug out in fear, yet are lifeless. My features are puffy and sallow. Twitches and tremors keep me in constant motion, yet I look immensely weighed down and immobile. No age is recognizable in my face or body. Everything is out of proportion, incongruous.

It is very frightening not to recognize oneself. I am not at home in my body. I exist in a barren land, wracked by upheaval, gouged and twisted, tortured by terrible storm.

I am a young country, being shaped and molded by the forces of life, caught up in the motions of destruction and rebirth.

· · · · · · ·

Lunch with an old friend today. As usual, with him, it was intense, rewarding, reassuring. He somehow believes in me, with few, if any, strings attached. And I can bathe in the warmth of his company without fear of manipulation, and in a reciprocal encounter that does not leave me drained.

How I hunger for companionship of that sort. If I could have just one friend, a buddy to play with, run or ski or just crazy adventure;

someone I could talk with intimately—back and forth; or, if female, someone I could also cuddle with, have sex with occasionally, without becoming inextricably intertwined.

Where to find such a woman? Is such a relationship possible for me? And why expect just one person to fill all those different needs?

The sex seems to muck it all up. I'm not able to just fuck someone occasionally and leave it at that. Yet sex is a very real need for me, and the person that I have sex with needs to be a person I am willing to engage with at all levels.

How to distinguish priorities? And am I even capable of such distinct deliberation as actively seeking a companion? And if found, conscious effort should be directed at nurturing that relationship into something healthy, without rushing forth in desperation, or holding back in fear and indecision.

I don't trust my judgment at this time! I am too reactive, too overloaded with feelings and confusion to make any clear statements. It is time for patience—time to wait quietly until what is trying to work itself out can resolve itself accordingly. My only actions now must be of self-nurturing. I am midway through a process of therapy which cannot be rushed or manipulated. I can only do my best not to inhibit it. I am glad to acknowledge my trust in it.

· · · · · · ·

I can see that my inability to concentrate, my absentmindedness and lack of peripheral attention are the result of a profound engagement—with myself—at a very deep level. It is consuming all of my energy, save the little bit required to get me through my days safely.

This is very good, what is happening. It is just so awkward and uncomfortable and intangible. And I can't help feeling that there must be some way to help it along. Yet I know that the best I can do is to make my life as tolerable as possible without inhibiting too much the process taking place.

The lethargy and nausea and toxicity and confusion are all extremely necessary. I recognize that there is a finite amount of it, and the more I can feel, the sooner it will be purged.

While some of the discomfort is surely the result of life at Zach's,

I am confident that most is the result of my body releasing those long-atrophied pockets of pain. And, perhaps, the trauma at Zach's is healthy, in its strange way intensifying my access to my pain.

And I also trust that I will assume no more than I am able to tolerate, and I can shut down whenever it gets to be too much. I have to trust myself in this.

My sensitivity to how much I can take, when to push and when to hold back, is maturing nicely, and is a wonderful attribute to have.

· · · · · · ·

Took the day off and went for a ski in the high country. Whenever I get off by myself, truly alone, the experience is never lonely. I never wish that there was someone else with me. When I clear my head of its diversions and distractions by going off alone somewhere wild, I am able to more clearly perceive my own being. Without the curtains of my defenses to hide it, my self can be accurately witnessed and experienced.

· · · · · · ·

Warm days now, with much solitude and free time to lounge around. But my finances are desperate right now, so my play must be approached frugally.

The most I can afford is to fill my car with gas and go for a hike or ski, but usually I spend my time reading, running, thinking, recovering from and preparing for the shock of Zach's.

· · · · · · ·

Saturday afternoon, cold and grey. Paul sits nestled in the rocks atop a mountain, looking out over a solemn, bleak landscape of endless hills, shrouded in pines and old snow. It is still, the silence broken only by an occasional bird. A storm moves in, obscuring the distance and filling me with existential loneliness.

Why, I wonder, do I seek out this solemn solitude, which weighs me down with despair and a profound sense of empty mortality? Why not stay in the city and surround myself with people and superficial distractions? What am I looking for?

In the grip of despair, at those times when he so acutely felt the need to somehow try to sort things out, Paul often seemed to be led to return to the Durango/Southwest Colorado setting. Near the end of winter, then, he found himself, again, among those familiar scenes, solitarily musing on the inner responses which they brought up.

Immersed in a world of black and white. Leaning against an aspen on a bare patch of ground at the mouth of the canyon below Molas Pass. Soaking up the poignant beauty of the simple shapes and contrasts of trees against snow against sky. My skis, upright in the snow, nod gently in the breeze. Fresh fox tracks crisscross the meadow before me.

My body is seized by a paralyzing melancholy. Alienated from the world of man, I find no empathy with the world of nature right now, either. Having lost access to the sense of my inner beauty, I may have also lost my ability to appreciate nature's beauty. I hope not.

· · · · · · ·

Familiarity strikes a chord as I sit in the park by the river in Durango. How many hundreds of hours have I sat here like this? How did it really feel back then? It seems like it was easier, more stable, more rewarding. It felt like home. I long for that feeling again, and I know that I'll never find my peace of mind in Denver; at times I wonder if I've ruined my life in moving there.

Perhaps what I have done in Denver is simply to extinguish my delusions. It does not seem impossible that I am inadequate for survival on this planet. My needs far outweigh my capabilities. My deficits as a human being can never be filled. The beauty of life is beyond my capacity to experience.

I have never known what it means to believe in myself, and I have survived thus far on other people's beliefs. But one cannot forever exist by watching other people eat.

Was Paul indeed "inadequate for survival on this planet"? No, I think it far more apt to consider that our society has somehow become unsuited for the Pauls among us. A very sad conclusion.

Cheesman Park in Denver again—feeling somewhat more calm. A rare treat, and probably the product of my week in Durango. The recent springtime weather is a factor too; I can resonate with the feelings of the earth and sense some life stirring inside, though still dormant.

When one lives one day at a time, incapable of comprehending tomorrow, and encountering sporadic and spontaneous fluctuations of a sense of being, then something like a little quiet sunshine has a profound effect on one's immediate reality. In another hour, who knows how I'll feel?

About to conclude his second year in Denver, in therapy, Paul sat down and, with superb clarity, summarized his situation—his understanding of what had happened, and the portents for his future. It is a revealing statement.

· · · · · · ·

As I once again read over the preceding months of entries, and their apparently discordant jumble of almost incoherent ramblings, I am nonetheless struck by the actual cohesiveness of my thoughts: how subtle bits and pieces from months back begin to accelerate in quantity and quality into a pattern of realization—building toward a turning point in my understanding.

Seemingly random statements or insights fall into place, soon to converge into a recognizable whole that is much more than the sum of its parts. A philosophical extrapolation building up steam with which to propel me into the next stage of my existence.

I am almost certain that this is not just a new expression or an experience of new feelings, but is instead the culmination of my past experience reaching some gestalt inside of me—a wisdom taking form, helped along by a reduction of resistance to, and a resolution of at least some of, the pain pushing on me.

It is a wisdom wrought with sorrow, though. As my delusions dissipate, the view that replaces that grey fog is not pretty, but at least

I can see where my paths may lie. It remains to be seen whether I have the strength and the resources to travel those paths.

After two long years in Denver, two years dedicated solely to feeling, at the expense of everything else, I have come to realize that, though I can recognize the potential value and beauty possible through Primal Therapy, it seems, for some unfathomable reason, unavailable to me. All I have been able to do is to obliterate the veil of ignorance which fills most people with hope, and I'm left with a very clear perspective of my own limitations, which are vast.

Instead of being the whole, clear being I have striven for, I must resign myself to accepting an understanding of the incomplete person I am, without the capacity to change that, and to try to design a life that circumnavigates my inadequacy and those things which cause me pain. That leaves me very little to work with.

Instead of reaching for some true, universal reality, where I may belong and coexist with everything, I have to limit myself to a reality conducive to my own limitations, filled with people and situations within my tolerances. Thus, I am no different than I was, except that now, all this must be done deliberately, and not unconsciously. An awesome task.

Now I am free to look forward; yet I cannot imagine what must come next. I haven't gained enough here; I've only managed to eradicate the willful stupidity which buffered me against the painful knowledge of my own reality. Hopefully, my burden will lessen some when I leave Denver, and shift my focus from feelings, and allow the wounds of my vulnerability to scar over—but I will always suffer from innate unhappiness; I will never experience light-heartedness; I will always be motivated by pain and desperation, rather than joy and ambition.

My solace lies in the fact that my life has been confronted honestly, my perceptions are true, and I have taken responsibility for myself to the furthest extent of my capabilities.

I guess that is how I would define a person's integrity.

If I'm lucky, I will someday stumble upon my home, and live out my life in relative complacency. And I'll die, having known who and what I was, and try to be satisfied with that wisdom. And if I die tomorrow, I will have that satisfaction.

Paul was once again drawn to Durango—to contemplate the past and its relationship with the present. And ahead?

At George's house near Durango, for a week of work and solitude. A new place, a new routine, a new set of values for a while. The quiet and the basic physical work do me good. The inner-penetration of isolation, though, consumes me with heartache.

In the moonlight I walk through dry pastures to the river's edge. It is a scene almost foreign to me. One that barely penetrates my attention. The stars look up at me from the water, a few elk rustle on the opposite bank, a mysterious animal drifts downstream and then dives when it notices me. And all I can do is sit and stare into that void which is my future.

. . . .

The wind has been blowing relentlessly all day, making work very difficult, stirring up my emotions. The agitation makes my tasks seem cruel and impossible to perform. Acknowledging the damage that might be done if I continue, I gratefully call a truce and stop for the day, and take the dogs for a walk up a small canyon to the east.

It brings back memories of other times in Durango. Sitting, looking out over the valley, I can see so many places where I've sat before in the late afternoon sun, alone—letting my mind wander, pondering my loneliness and my incomprehensible existence.

My mind is awash with memories as of late: lovers, friends, places I've been and places I've dreamed—during a time, though humble in its depth, when I was past the pain of my childhood, and having yet to experience the despair of recognizing the responsibility for my life. Something has changed which makes it seem that simple pleasure is beyond my grasp now. The memories return when I am doing things which I have done before, which once brought me joy, and are now just empty excursions into my own anguish.

I wonder why I write only of my own personal feelings? I have so many insights in the course of a day that I would like to record, some very deep and sensitive observations about the world around me. Yet because they are not concerning me, they seem peripheral, and without true value. Another example of my tragic isolation, my irrevocable alienation from the world at large.

. . . .

Time to leave Durango. It's time to come back to earth. Time to *live* life and quit trying so desperately to *understand* it. A thankless, futile and unrewarding task, it seems. The complexity of life is far beyond my capacity to comprehend; the best I can do is to grant it the respect that it deserves, and to maybe learn to enjoy the sanctuary of my ignorance. Live, if I can, in blind bliss, and let the answers present themselves if and when they will.

It's a big enough challenge just to survive in this world. Why squander my energy with such elusive, esoteric bumbling? Better to use it learning how to survive gracefully.

. . . .

Feeling very good tonight; sitting in the grasses beneath a breezy spring night. Thinking back, fantasizing about past times.

The high points of my life have all focused on women, it seems, and as I sit snuggled into the intimate darkness, I am overcome by a sense of warmth and gratitude at the thought of certain incidents from my past. The feelings are as real and alive as when they first occurred.
• my first day with Marie, at Big Sur.
• crawling into Cindy's bed with flowers and wine.
• making love to Dawn.

But the richest, most loving, passionate, acute memories are of Jenny—my very first lover. The whole experience with her, when remembered bit by bit, floods my senses with a feeling close to rapture. My body and consciousness start to melt from the heat of those images.

I would do anything to see her again.

. . . .

It is very late at night. I lie naked upon my bed, beneath open windows. The world is asleep, but not I.

I lie, enraptured by the seductive sound of the rain, embraced by its warmth and its wetness, and its soft whispering.

I find myself drifting quietly away, upon my little boat of fantasy.

. . . .

Something akin to complacency begins to permeate my being now; a lightheartedness takes hold which is very surprising, and enormously reassuring. A calmness warms my heart; gracefulness and agility return to my body and to my thoughts; a sense of comfort and of confidence propels me along.

The transformations occurring now seem massive; by changing the situations in which I engage, how I spend my time, and with whom, how I earn my keep—somehow this has created a transformation in me at a very basic level. I am certainly relieved to be done with Zach's. I am once again at home with myself. Something I haven't felt for a very long time.

I hope that it is not something temporary, but a true change that will forever be with me in some form. I am able to perceive the impact that Primal Therapy has had on me; it is enormous, delightful, profound.

My work with Sam, in helping build a beautiful house, is rewarding and healthy. I feel very much in control of my abilities, and am learning and growing in a satisfying way. I am proving that I can make my own way. People once again respond to me in a warm, and often exciting, manner. My creativity once again unfolds, and life seems important, and fulfilling.

I still have no specific future, but I have a sense of possibility. I have more of myself than ever before, and it no longer feels totally impossible that I may achieve satisfaction and peace of mind.

Perhaps this is a new beginning. Perhaps I will start to live now. Finally.

. . . .

I gaze into the mirror, and am able to recognize my reflection. Like an old friend come home, or a dormant love, reawakening, I am

no longer a stranger to myself. I sense the power inherent in a human being: myself.

Along the long road that I travel alone, I have left the wintertime of the bleak desert, and find myself in a green valley of life in abundance. Perhaps I'll camp here for a while.

> The blind bird has opened its eyes,
> and a new song trembles in its throat.

Moving On

The Twenty-ninth Year

An appropriate day to begin a new journal: empty and clear, unblemished, full of potential and anticipation.

I certainly hope that this chapter can be more peaceful than the last. If words had any real power, the writings of the last year or so would have eaten right through the paper, the cover, probably even the table I chanced to lay my journal upon—so wrought with anxiety were those words.

So, today marks twenty-eight years of life on this earth, in this body, out on my own.

I wonder if I'll see another twenty-eight? I wonder how it will feel then? We're certainly not guaranteed happiness, but we sure feel like we deserve it. I know I do.

It's such a strange existence we humans have. I wonder if I'd trade it for another, if I had the chance? I doubt it. This is what I am. In whatever form it took, it would be my basic, deepest essence which determined the flavor of my life. That can never be changed. I can only find more creative, more pleasant ways to accommodate my spirit, to express my being. But it is there, as is, for better or worse. I cannot quantitatively change it. I can only accept, or deny it.

. . . .

Steamboat Springs—a short holiday.

The recent days of exhilaration fade into melancholy. It makes me wonder. The joy is so unstable—the sadness so severe.

The human imagination is one of the most beautiful of mysteries, but it can be so deceiving. It opens up the spectrum of perception three-hundred-sixty degrees, beyond time and space, beyond everything but the most translucent reality.

Perhaps the present is too contained for a man, too confining a concept.

. . . .

High atop a rock at the edge of Zirkel Wilderness, gazing into the interior of a wild, yet gentle, paradise. The Dome and Lost Ranger Peak stare down at me from afar. It's all so familiar; this was my home, and I am deeply touched to be here once again.

In the story of my life, this represents the turning point. My experiences here were my first of beauty, love, and personal power. I would never have survived this far if I hadn't succumbed to the gentle peace of the wild. I would never have known of reality.

. . . .

The first day of summer: the days roll by me, thump thump thump, like the rails beneath a train. Endlessly repetitious, but somehow soothing, seductive and trance-like. The extreme angles of up and down wear away, and I roll along like some smooth, soft ball. Existing. Maintaining. Dull. Developing a crust of boredom, an envelope of lethargy.

. . . .

Nothing seems to matter except for my relentless hunger for a quiet stream, somewhere far away, sitting below a tree in the quiet breeze, alone.

Nothing seems to touch me now as I rock listlessly along on the swells of humble dissatisfaction. I desire nothing more than I desire solitude, undisturbed.

The petty anxieties and awkwardness—the irresolute, discordant hum of panic seem like an irritating arthritis of my heart, tragically crippling, in a meek sort of way. But not enough to kill me. There is no passion to my suffering.

. . . .

There are still these times when I am unable to separate myself from my feelings. It's not as if something happens which triggers an increase in ascending pain; it's more as if too much occurs to incorporate, and my system goes into an overload in which my resistance is nullified. The circuit breaker is thrown— but not before a power surge of irresolute emotion floods my system, permeating my being with unrestrained feeling, and throwing my tolerance modifiers into shock.

This would all be fascinating, were my life more stable, my sense of self more intact. Fascinating because of the intense barrage of symbolism my poor mind creates in its desperate attempt to make sense of, to give form to, this onslaught of indefinable expression.

Instead, it is very frightening. My hold on life seems so delicate, so tentative. When the little power of clarity and organization which I possess is stripped away, I feel myself being sucked down a whirlpool of nonsense and reaction, where nothing is connected, there are no rules of cause and effect, no coherent basis for judgment or decisions. I am swept away on the turbulent floodwaters of emotion.

My most tangible dream at the moment would involve moving to Durango, finding a small place by the river, working in architecture, falling in love, having lots of time to play and wander, saving some bucks, settling in. In a sense, starting over, with a realistic, deliberate scheme to my life.

But, truly, I haven't the slightest idea what may happen. I haven't many clues or inclinations. I feel a strong pull to wander off by myself into the woods for a while, perhaps on horseback. But I sense that this may be some not-quite-appropriate expression of some feeling simmering away deep within—my parasympathetic nervous system filling me with juices which stimulate an acute need to run away, far away, to where I know it's safe and I have only my own loneliness to contend with.

But other than the peace and clarity of mind to be gained from such an innocuous solitude, such a move would provide only temporary relief, and I would still have to return to a big gnawing question: what am I going to do with myself for the next fifty years? How am I going to put some substantial form to my life? When, if ever, will I be able to pull myself out of these self-indulgent eddies and into the mainstream current of existence? Will there ever come a time when I am able to drop this unnecessary load and dance off down the trail? When will I finally begin to be alive, without all of this squandering, this waste, of the human spirit?

. . . .

Early morning at one of my favorite settings in the forest. Quiet and somber after an evening of magnificent, relentless thunderstorm. Clouds sweep restlessly among the valleys, like rivers searching for a lost sea.

Birds and squirrels and other undefinable forms of life are hesitant to start the day, for they can see the ominous threat of still more storms hovering above the periphery of the horizon, enveloping the world in a shroud of dark satin. All around lies the blatant expression of a power too great to incorporate.

People in the world around me go about the business of maintaining their shallow and demented realities, performing the meaningless and habitual rituals of the morning—without any awareness that today, as always, is different from any other day.

And I, as usual, am stuck somewhere in the middle, with no pacifying rituals of my own to anesthetize the fear.

. . . .

Back in Denver now, passing time in my usual ways. Too many feelings arise to live constructively, but I seem unable to resolve this blanket of despair which is suffocating my spirit. Spent the night with Sally, which was sweet, but I seem unable to let go. I cannot open up my heart and engage with any sense of compassion. I distrust myself and my own motivations too much to believe another's—to accept that someone else would like to be with me regardless of my discrepancies and weaknesses.

Still, I welcome the acknowledgment, if only because of my physical appearance or my attentions in bed. I am badly in need of nurturing, and will take whatever support I can get, if it is at all sincere.

It is obviously time to work within a new context. The people and places I am involved with are no longer appropriate, and I can feel myself being damaged.

I don't want to live here; I don't want to work here. Yet I seem unable to create a better situation. I am frightened by the degree to which I've shut down. My sensitivity, creativity, inspiration and compassion are hidden away.

. . . .

Once again the time has come for making major decisions, major transitions. As usual, the signs have been blatantly apparent for a long, long time. Yet, I've lacked the impetus to set things directly in motion by myself, so someone else is needed to force my hand, usually at the cost of an important relationship. I never seem to feel ready, well prepared or strong enough. I always slip through by a shoestring, leaving too much unresolved, and not enough anticipated.

It's time for me to leave Denver. I could find reason enough to stay, but it's all based on fear. So the question is, if it's time to take some risks, how big a risk am I able to tolerate? What soon becomes apparent is my opaque sense of direction. If I really had a purpose, no risk would be too great, for I would have the internal wherewithal to achieve my chosen goal. It seems, though, that decisions and risks are forced upon me without my approval, thus creating a sense of incomprehensible panic.

Will I never feel a sense of control over my life, or will it come too late? Everything feels like a nonsensical accident. At least I'm not paranoid to the point of thinking that other people are doing things to me. Is direction just the product of coincidental choice?

The major pull is toward breaking all ties and starting over somewhere else. But have I the resources, or is that a denial of all that I've lived before? All that I've built for myself?

Where does the greatest responsibility lie?

Paul eventually decided to leave Denver, with a new lover, Julie—not very confidently—but with no other good options in sight. I would miss having him near, but I knew that it was inevitable. This change in locale did not work out very well, though, nor last very long.

The incoherency of my actions and perceptions makes this sort of self-dialogue seem irrelevant and unsubstantial; yet there is also a sense of urgency in coming to terms with what is happening.

The fear of survival is overwhelming, yet in my graceless fashion, I maintain. In a few weeks I move to Aspen, into a tentative and ill-formed situation, with a woman I barely know, yet seem to trust completely. With little overt definition of my own, I am left to depend on my frail faith, and with much trepidation, simply allow these strange circumstances to run their course.

. . . .

Aspen after a month; I find it interesting and somewhat tantalizing, but somehow not at all consistent with what I need to be doing.

The strength of my resistance to the situation implies a deep and urgent attempt to avoid catastrophe, rather than any sort of apathy based on fear or laziness.

I do not feel prompted to take advantage of the environment, as I usually do. I turn down jobs, truly rare commodities in this town, even though my financial situation is borderline. I alienate myself from a beautiful woman who would assure me of sensitive and fulfilling companionship. Why?

Somehow I sense that I'm violating myself right now by living in close proximity, geographically (but primarily emotionally) with other people. I have an incredible hunger to be basically alone someplace new and far away where no one knows me.

Would I survive on my own?

. . . .

This Sunday afternoon finds me sitting in absolute silence, above Aspen, on a south slope in incredible sunlight, overlooking an unbelievable landscape of snow-covered peaks, crags and pinnacles, cirques and bowls, and just basic raw immensity.

After several miles of gradual climbing, I look down on my reward: acres of steep unbroken snowfields. I sit on a stump, drinking Irish coffee, stoking my fires for the descent.

Now, even more than ever before, these too-occasional excursions into the wild seem to be the only experiences with any reward, any sense of reality, any sort of resonance with my internal being. It is tragic to live a life where only a few hours every week really have any impact, really seem to matter.

I do not understand why it is so difficult for me to find or create an environment and a lifestyle which is in synch with my needs. My resistance right now is overwhelming, and it is real. My innate intelligence is denying any acceptance of what is happening. I cannot justify my existence in its present form. I am tired of compromise.

. . . .

Dad,

It's very still today, cold, grey, and snowing heavily. Not a good day to spend working—far too long and weighted with introspection. I am overcome by feelings that will not be denied: fetal feelings that I sense in my teeth, amorphous images that I can't quite place, but yet are so familiar. So I call in sick, although the truth is so much the opposite, and well worth the sacrifice that a day's pay means to me right now. As usual.

I only hope that I can take advantage of the opportunity for reality, when it presents itself so powerfully, so seductively, so almost . . . ? It seems so seldom that life gives us what we have earned.

I have found Aspen to be a grave disappointment, although I have learned some valuable lessons in the short time that I've been here. It's so hard to find a place that fits, but perhaps I'm too particular, or selfish, or just confused. I can no longer compromise, even for survival's sake.

Happiness seems but a distant star, but perhaps peace of mind will one day be mine. I am trying the best that I know how. Yet my life is so full of tears.

Just wanted to say thanks for your support lately. I feel that you have an understanding of the depth and the sincerity of the decisions being made, in spite of how awkward and irresponsible they must appear from the outside.

Your very special sensitivity does not go unnoticed.

Nor unappreciated.

I love you,
Paul

Dear Paul,

My several visits to Aspen and our phone conversations make me, as always, extremely proud that you are my son. I appreciate, as perhaps no one else ever could, the intensity, the integrity, the perseverance which you continue to summon.

Where the strength and inspiration for such an effort ultimately comes from, I can only wonder, and wonder. But at the crucial times, they seem to appear, and we are most fortunate for that. No, I don't view your decisions as awkward nor irresponsible. You have my total admiration—and love.

Dad

Last Days
The Start of Another Year

Paul decided to leave Aspen and Julie, and return to Durango.

But first, during one final trip to California, came a short, poignant letter from him that stunned me with its complete rightness and eloquence. In a note which took me perhaps two minutes to read, and not much longer for him to write—in just these brief sentences he seemed to summarize himself more totally and successfully than ever before. It defined his life, his deepest holdings, and his most troublesome confusions, all succinctly, and tenderly.

I cannot read it without tears coming.

Hello my friend,

It is nightfall at Deetjen's Big Sur Inn, and the moon is chasing the sun out across the Pacific. I am content, tired and sated, after a solitary meal by the fireplace, and a day of quiet adventure.

An early breakfast on the deck in the fog, some quiet time with my journal. Then a few hours of timeless exploration along a creek winding through the mist-enshrouded forests to the east.

When the sun finally loosed itself, I made a treacherous descent down the cliffs, to the hidden beach where the sea lions congregate by

182

the hundreds. Remember? There I took off my clothes and crawled through the sand and rocks, like something out of a spy movie, getting very close to those huge, sea-smoothed beasts, listening carefully to their grunts and sighs and whisperings.

Then a few hours, sitting on a little hand-hewn bench nestled in the hillside above the inn, gazing out across the sea with my binoculars, watching the slow deliberate progress, the spouts and undulations of the whales, moving serenely northward.

Then, when the fog obscures the sea once again I lose myself, beneath a redwood tree beside a stream, in the chapters of a book.

This is the closest I can come to feeling alive, and yet I am restless and sad, knowing this is so transitory, so temporary, so elusive and unreal, in a worldly sense.

All I really ask from life is to be allowed to wander through unknown forests, wading through crystalline creeks or foamy surf, watching the sun move across the sky, or the birds. Exploring the thighs of beautiful, lonely women, or floating peacefully through my dreams at night.

My needs are simple, yet so naive. There is no place in the world for a life like that: the machinery of civilization does not tolerate such slothfulness and irresponsibility, such lack of ambition.

It is quite a dilemma: I know that for me, to work for a living, day after day, is poison to my system, and will kill me, quite literally, in a short time. I can acknowledge that truth, and hunger for a different, more innocuous, way of life, but I cannot comprehend a resolution; I cannot imagine how to create an existence in this world today that satisfies my need for solitude, for spontaneity, for introspection, for the pure and unadulterated experience of nature's beauty.

I must sacrifice my spirit for survival's sake, and yet. . . .

I cannot. I resist that unreality with every cell of my body, and it causes in me a great sickness.

Every day I must compromise so much. For what? I can make no sense of it.

Yours, in beauty and in sadness.

Paul

In Denver, I had formed a most promising and rewarding relationship with a new mate, and we were exploring the possibility of relocating near Durango and building a house there. It would be a welcome relief from life in the city—and a new opportunity to live near my son. We all looked forward to the prospect.

As Paul moved back, once again, to Durango—his favorite setting—he was able to crystallize inside himself, it seems to me, the truths that he held most dear—that he trusted most highly. He concluded that he lived in a world in which he did not fit; that all of his efforts to find a way, with integrity, to do so had not worked; that his fond connection with the outdoors, with nature, showed him most clearly what the real really consisted of; and that there was no chance of reconciling these.

Dad,

Early afternoon, Southwest Coffee House, Durango. It's a dreary, drizzly day; a somber day, a day for sitting beneath a tree beside the river. There is no time for that sort of thing, though, so I sit here and shore up my defenses with caffeine, creating an anxious initiative that allows me to make my phone calls, to smile cheerfully and intelligently at strangers who, for some incomprehensible reason, seem to have some control over my survival.

Durango has, at least for now, lost much of its comfort for me. It seems to be an adversary, formidable and intimidating. Floundering in the midst of an economic depression, its citizens are lethargic and full of fear. It is with great uncertainty that I can anticipate succeeding in my efforts here.

Lacking both the blind optimism and the detached creativity which might produce or discover that perfect hidden situation, I must rely on subtler, more obscure, and seemingly less effective avenues for finding my place here. My clarity of purpose is clouded by a frustrating sense of resignation and futility.

It would be so tempting to rush back to the warmth and security of life with Julie; I cannot be certain that that wouldn't be the right thing to do.

Still, there are some obvious advantages to being here. It is a *real* place, its inhabitants living lives of humble integrity. I have many friends here, and I find so rewarding the opportunity to once again share in another's company, conversation, thoughts and feelings. Spring is arriving, and I can find comfort in a very familiar sort of beauty—an experience that I can actually make some sense of.

I spent some time at your new homesite. What an extraordinary place. I do not question that you have made a very good decision to move there; you will find a very good life waiting for you. Hopefully my own reputation in this town will serve you well in your endeavor to establish yourself there. That would mean a lot to me. I send greeting from several of our mutual friends.

Paul

Dear Paul,

Both the pains and pleasures of your new situation shine through your words with great clarity.

One of the brightest spots in my present consciousness is the anticipation of once again living very close to you, especially the prospect of working together on our new house. Yes, it is a superb setting and I'm optimistic about our being able to create just the right design for that home in the woods, with your inputs. You truly are one of the most creative people I've known.

I wish you well in your searching there, and expect to be able to see you again soon.

Love,
Dad

. . . .

Paul did establish a home in Durango; he found a "satisfactory" job; he renewed old friendships—but, deep inside, he knew that these motions did not add up to rightness. Even so, he persisted in his search, painful and confusing as it was.

Dad,

Spent a few hours today sitting in a very familiar spot: beneath an ancient piñon pine on a carpet of spring grasses, above Waterfall Ranch, at the edge of the meadows that look out on the sandstone

185

cliffs that tower above. Andy and I used to sit here a lot, discussing the awkwardness and the beauty of our young lives.

The place has lost none of its mystery or sense of the sublime, its power to calm and clarify. If one believes in archetypal spirits, they certainly influence this space. There are powers much more alive than the human spirit residing here. You have found a perfect place to live your life. I look forward to exploring its beauty with you.

My hunger for solitude, for wandering and quiet adventure, grows stronger. I am unable to stifle that need in deference to the more pragmatic and acute business of survival.

Still, Durango is treating me well, in spite of the anxiety of finances and worldly organization. My gentleness returns, the seeds of creativity tremble with anticipation.

It may take a while, but with patience, I may find myself at home with myself once again. Soon, I hope. It has been too long.

Just wanted to tell you how much I love you, and appreciate your participation in my life.

Paul

. . . .

Another day of quiet solitary wandering.

Out of all of the confusion of life, this is the one thing that makes absolute and very easy sense to me. Although most of my life seems to exist as an attempt by God to reassure me of my humility, I find nothing humble in my earthly explorations. The ego is not involved in wandering along a creek or up an unknown pathway through the forest. Only the spirit can participate in such things.

For that reason, Durango is a good place for me to be. It lies nestled in the cradle of an endless and gentle landscape, filled with gentle people who seem to be so by virtue of their proximity to such overwhelming beauty. I'm hoping that some of that beauty and some of that gentleness will rub off on me. I am surely in need of it.

. . . .

Today I sit high atop the cliffs of a box canyon. I have finally found my elusive waterfall, and am delighted to have fulfilled that

186

goal, as simple as it seems. It is nice to know that I can persist when there is something that I really want.

There is not much survival, I suppose, in pursuing situations of beauty, but it is the only thing that seems real to me. It alone assures me that I am a viable human being.

Perhaps it is just escape, though. I am frighteningly concerned with what is going to become of me. I seem to grow more and more incapable of coping with daily existence. I have no more idea of, and a lot less ability to facilitate, what I want to do with my life, than I did when I slid out of the womb almost twenty-nine years ago. In spite of my supposed sincerity, I live a pathetically superficial life. I can still find very little to respect about myself.

Perhaps I just don't care.

. . . .

Turtle Lake now. A spot very dear to my heart. In all of the places of wonder within close proximity to Durango, this is undoubtedly my favorite. The water, the wildlife, the incredible birdsong, the very sensual horizon lines—it is just the right combination for me.

I really wish that I had something meaningful to say, something poignant, perhaps even joyful. But there is a great emptiness that lies within and about me. Like the husk of a frog that has been sucked dry by a giant water bug. The shape remains, intact, but vacant; suspended in time, but soon to suddenly fold in on itself and disintegrate.

All the lights on, but nobody home.

I desperately need some outside force to take hold of me and propel me out of this void. Always before it has been a lover who supplied that inspiration, that fresh information. But one cannot count on such occurrences, and for me, it always means assuming another person's reality, not any nurturing of my own. And that seems to just enunciate my own self-denial.

All of my years of self-exploration seem to have led to an empty desert—lifeless and vacant.

. . . .

Memorial Day—a gorgeous spring day, lounging on a sunny sandbar next to Junction Creek; a gentle sun complements the violent chattering of the water.

I find myself alone again after a few weeks of constant visitors. Dad, Julie, Molly, Andy and June, Les and Alli. It's been nice; certainly saved me from various forms of starvation. But I wasn't very touched by most of it. I'm amazed at how frighteningly apathetic I've become. Perhaps it's just a product of therapy, but the old friends and old ways just don't interest me anymore. Probably, though, it's just a lack of passion—a deadening of my senses and curiosity. I seem more concerned with simply passing time as comfortably as possible, and even that is a chore.

It's funny. Andy asked me what I was searching so hard for, and the only answer I could come up with was comfort. I just want to be comfortable with myself. Nothing very esoteric about that.

I don't at all like the way things are going. It seems, sometimes, that my failure in life is almost complete. I have exhausted my life's energy and never even reached first base. I bunt, pathetically, in the most innocuous situations, always wishing that the pitcher will walk me to home base. In fact, I am so intimidated by the game, most times I would prefer to strike out quickly and get it over with.

What little pride I have remaining is used up in hiding from the magnitude of my shame. Success is no longer a possibility. What I'd like to know is: was it ever?

My Dear Son,

My recent visit meant a lot to me, as always. Your new home, your job, your reunion with old friends: it all has a good feel to it. I appreciate your hospitality—all your attentions to me.

And yet, I sense also your sadness. You're still engaged, I know, in that long search for rightness, and it is terribly elusive, isn't it? It's a mighty strange world we're asked to live in, and I hope with all my heart for your success in this quest. No one ever deserved it more.

Love,
Dad

. . . .

I was getting increasingly concerned over what I thought I saw in my son. He certainly continued to share his affection, some of his more profound thoughts, and a little of his playfulness with me. But at a deeper level, he seemed to be drawing back inside himself, keeping a kind of reserve—or was it resignation?

I wasn't sure what to call it, and I wasn't alarmed about it, yet. He was still himself, after all . . . almost. But it was sobering to witness his struggling.

Had I been aware of the thoughts being confided to his journal at this time, I would have been much more disturbed, apprehensive, afraid.

Leaning against a pinnacle of rock high above Junction Creek. The luminous, voluptuous white rock flows down around me in all directions, finally disappearing into the dense forest below.

I sit here and think of the rock covered with blood—my blood—flowing down the porous rock, staining it red forever.

This would be a good place to die: a powerful place, frightening in its wildness. Exposed to the elements, to the sky all around, to the endless horizons. A powerful spot for a powerful act. An honest statement, a fitting finale.

Once again I find myself backed against that impenetrable barrier, where all my thoughts turn to death. It seems so obviously the proper thing to do, unquestionably the most appropriate response to my life's situation.

Yet, it is an act which I don't seem to have the strength for. I am so pathetically weak-willed. There is no hope, in any direction.

. . . .

A too-warm but still enjoyable Sunday afternoon beneath a tree in a park by the river. Listless and lethargic after a long and exciting night of socializing with a dear old group of friends. I enjoy their valuable company, but I wish it didn't need to take place within the confines of a noisy bar. The music and conversation is a treat, but as usual I overindulge in drinking in order to pump up my charisma, and lose all sensitivity and appreciation for the encounters that take place.

I don't understand just how much honesty is expressed by the character which asserts itself when I drink. I don't like that person very much, but his appearance is so desperate and spontaneous that I fear there is a great deal of truth in the emotions which are displayed. It is not that it is unattractive; I'm sure there is a great deal of charm portrayed. But I would wish for more integrity and depth. I fear I am letting down those people who have believed in me in the past. Perhaps I really am doing a lethal nose-dive toward an ugly death.

Today, at age twenty-nine, I am awed by the degree of unhappiness and dissatisfaction which I experience. It seems to be hopelessly chronic, and growing daily. I have almost no understanding of what it is that I'm struggling with, but the force of it alone is unbelievable and so frightening; I expend all of my strength doing battle with that fear, and never break through to the real confrontation.

At this point, as lost as I am in my confusion, and responding as I do in such a debilitating way, I would have to say that I have no future at all; and I make sure to discourage any reliance on, or involvement with me by, anyone who might be deluded into thinking otherwise.

The bottom line is that I have absolutely no idea, in any way, of what is going on in my life. There is no point of reference on which to base my reality; thus there is no possibility for action, but only reaction.

Penned on a birthday card to me:

Dad,

I'm glad that the music of your life can be so light-hearted and full of joy and passion.

You've earned it—and much more . . . .

> I love you,
> Paul

I visited Paul in Durango one more time that summer. The memories of those days are still vivid within me: seeing his work as a carpenter, and sharing lunch with him at the construction site of an elegant new house; running into him at a barn dance hosted by mutual friends, where I was again struck by how truly beautiful he was; having him join me at dinner the next evening, after which he left early, and quietly.

It was the last time I ever saw my son—and is perhaps the most intense of all my images of him.

Playing beside a creek in the hot afternoon sun; splashing in the water, chasing trout, skipping stones, swatting flies.

This is my kind of life, as simple as it sounds. And very much appreciated, after weeks of agonizing anxiety and discomfort.

I seem to be fighting my life every step of the way—finding nothing that satisfies me, nothing to make me respect my life.

If I were free to do anything I'd like right now, I think I would move out to the ocean, buy a kayak and a guitar, and spend my days playing in the waves, and my nights making music. Perhaps I'd learn how to dive too, and fly. I'd probably even go back to school. My second choice would be to settle down with a woman that I love, and make a home.

Both scenarios seem to be far, far out of my reach. Seems I'm always wishing for what might be, and despising what really is.

And yet I continue to dream. For who knows what lies beyond the next hill? Another desert, a cold and harsh mountain range or, perhaps, the ocean.

My home, at last?

Leaving . . . and Looking Back

An Epilogue

S*hortly after this last journal entry, Paul walked into the forest, up to that lovely spot which he had described earlier as a good place to die, and while listening to some of his favorite music and gazing out over that final, late summer evening scene, of vast wild beloved beauty, he ended his life. As with most everything he did, he accomplished this act with care and grace—thoughtfully.*

Earlier in the day he had written me his last letter:

Dad,

This is to say good-bye. It's time. I am broken into too many pieces.

I would have liked to have done this in a more graceful way, and to have tied together the loose ends of my life, so that my leaving would not be so traumatic for those around me. But I cannot wait. I cannot tolerate another day of pain.

I do not understand why life hurts me so badly. I've tried so hard to change that, but a person has only so much he can do, and I've used it up. There is no more hope. I can see clearly that all I have to look forward to is a life of more pain and discomfort. That will never change.

So, I feel that this is the most appropriate response to that situation. There is no other resolution. Vincent van Gogh once said that sadness lasts a lifetime. I would add that the sorrow grows deeper every day, for those of us who have been cursed with the sensitivity to comprehend what is, and the imagination to perceive how it should have been.

I deeply regret causing you this pain. You, above anyone else, have loved me, understood me, given me the most. And you will be the one most capable of accepting this very difficult decision which I have had to make. Perhaps now, I will finally attain the peace of mind which I have hungered for so relentlessly.

Please take good care of Leslie and Allison; they certainly deserve it.

I love you all very dearly, and am so sorry that it has to end this way. But it is for the best.

Good-bye.

Paul

After I received the news, I could only agonize in my journal:

There is no sense, let alone any justice, in this strange life. Paul was, without doubt, the finest person I ever knew. My best friend. Why his life was so much pain and despair is not explainable.

Except, this so-called civilization of ours is so unnatural and out-of-tune, that when one of its members is closer to the real, the true, he cannot fit in. He was thwarted at most every turn.

He tried valiantly, resourcefully, to redirect the path; he couldn't. And so, he's gone now.

Good-bye my son, good-bye. I loved you.

. . . .

Seven years earlier, Paul had observed:

I've spent a lot of thought and imagination on the questions of aging, and the grace and fluidness to be anticipated in later years. Thinking that I could live halfway into the twenty-first century is mind boggling, and what this does to my attitude toward the now is rather refreshing. And yet, I don't know if it's just me, or if it's all around me, but people sure seem to be in a horrendous hurry to get an awful lot done. (Like the pressure to grow up.) And of course this doesn't work; it merely compounds the problem. It makes things even more meaningless than they already are, and we find ourselves doing things for reasons totally unrelated to their real purpose or nature.

Our greatest waste now is people: our personal power, community power, human power. We exhaust ourselves with such futile, meaningless efforts—all the while placing incredible importance on every motion we go through. No wonder I feel worn and threadbare at twenty-two. Realizing that I might live another sixty years, one hundred years even, eases that pressure a little, but not completely.

For even if I were to die halfway through this sentence, I should feel that there is, and has been, time enough.

Recently, in a dream, I came upon Paul, hiking one of his favorite mountain trails. He nodded hello; I nodded back. We walked together in silence for a while—each of us savoring the simple sweetness of nature. He looked wonderful: wise, content, lighthearted even. Presently, he turned and said:

Dad, all of my earlier confusion and despair has lifted. It's so much better for me here; I can see clearly that that world wasn't really suited for me. Strange how we humans have drifted, generation after generation, further and further from any natural kind of life—any life we were truly equipped for. Made it very difficult for some of us to find our way—a right way.

If I could only have trusted my self—my insides—just a little more back then, I might have made it . . . but I knew too much—and yet, not quite enough. The coyotes and the eagles, the whales and the trees, they really have been more aware than we—right along. I've gotten to know a few of them quite well; they didn't lose their way like we did. I think you understand.

Now I'm going to take this steeper trail to the right; if you continue to the left, there's a great view just ahead up there. So, my journey continues—and so does yours. We'll talk again the next time we meet. Until then, adios.